Telehealth, Telemedicine or Electronic Health Simplified:

Telehealth, Telemedicine or Electronic Health Simplified:

❖

A Quick Guide for the General Public and Professionals

Dr. Joan Emeli-Komolafe

New York, United States of America

To order additional copies of this book, contact:
Xlibris LLC
1-888-795-4274
www.Xlibris.com
Orders@Xlibris.com
552677

CONTENTS

This book is dedicated to God for his mercies;
through him, all things are possible.

ACKNOWLEDGMENTS

Thanks to my family and friends for their support in helping me become the person that I am today. My mother, Princess Theresa Akinyooye-Emeli; my father, Chief Victor Emeli; my late aunt, Dr. Cecilia Emeli, and my husband, Joseph Komolafe Sr. Love to all my children, Joseph Jr., Dr. Grace Komolafe, my assistant and co-editor, Michael, and Joan Kmolafe Jr. my co-editor. Million appreciations to my former bosses, Regina Hawkey; Theodora Johnston, who assigned me to a telehealth project that enhanced my interest in telehealth; and my mentor and co-editor, Gloria Prince. Your patience and understanding means the world to me.

PREFACE

A simple introduction of the wonderful and cost effective world of Tele-health to the general public; and quick resource for professionals.

TELEHEALTH, TELEMEDICINE OR ELECTRONIC HEALTH WHAT'S IN A NAME? DOES IT MATTER?

What is in a name? Plenty if it has to do with your health; humongous if it has to do with life-and-death situations.

As we continue to debate the issues of health care in our nation, I began to explore some of the very funny moments I observed and not-so-funny consequences of the drama that is unfolding and is being played out on our national televisions, our political capital, our streets, our homes, and by our politicians and our citizens.

Names and identities are often given for a reason. Without a name or identity, we are all beings roaming this earth. Let's imagine for a moment a world where no names or identities are attached to anything. Imagine waking up and all your family members, friends, pets, things, etc., have no names, no identity. Imagine how chaotic your day would start off. You walk into a hospital full of patients with no identities, no names, a nursery full of newborns with no names, no identities, a home-care setting full of home-care patients with no names, no identities. I am sure that you are getting the drift by now. Yes, chaos would ensue, to say the least. Now you get the gist as to why we are so attached to the idea of *names* and *identities*. Yes, we name and identify people and things for a reason. Identities are given to people and things for a very good reason.

Depending on your culture, there are also meanings attached to naming and identifying people and things. Some cultures observe a child and choose a name that suits that child's personality. When Kate, the Duchess of England, and Prince William named their newborn child George the III, it was suggested that the name was chosen due to several reasons as reported below.

The Naming Connections

On July 24, 2013, Prince William and Kate, the Duchess of Cambridge, named their first son George Alexander Louis. This was two days after Kate delivered their first son at St. Mary's Hospital, London. The name George was not chosen at random, as you will see in the following speculations as explained by *E! Online,* July 26, 2013.

The speculation was that there were many circumstances surrounding the choosing of the name George Alexander Louis by the royal couple.

- The first speculation was that the name was chosen for the traditional, classic, historic connotation.
- The second speculation was that the name was chosen to honor Queen Elizabeth II's father.
- The third speculation was that the name was chosen as an ode to Prince William's late mother, Princess Diana.
- It was stated that Princess Diana had three nephews, named George, Alexander, and Louis. It was reported that in 1994, Diana's brother Charles had a son named Louis Frederick John Spencer I, and her sisters, Sarah and Jane, gave birth to sons named George Edmund and Alexander Robert respectively.
- The fourth speculation was the Prince Charles connection. It was speculated that the Duchess of Cambridge and Prince William chose the name George because of Prince William's fascination with late king George III who ruled England from 1760 to 1820. Prince William thought he was a very good king who led England through tough times like the social upheaval, Industrial Revolution, and terrible hardship inflicted on England by sixty years of war with Napoleon. Despite the fact that history labeled him as a mad king, Prince William viewed him as a really good king (*E! Online* July 26, 2013, retrieved 11/3/2013).

Now let's get back to the question of what's in a name.

The explanations above are used as an illustration of how names are chosen, why names matter, why we need to understand how the perception of a chosen name can make or break our agenda, and why we should take time to understand the action and reaction, or lack of action and reaction, behind a chosen name.

I am certain Prince William and Kate Middleton took some of the above reasoning into consideration in choosing the name of their little prince. The belief in some cultures is that the names are given based on the child's characteristics or the name would determine the child's character and shape his or her future. Some cultures or families have a tradition of naming a child after a deceased family member. It could be a father, a mother, a grandparent, an aunt or uncle, or even siblings. Often, these traditions are meant to give hope to the family, honor the deceased family member, comfort the family, or just a way to follow a tradition set by their ancestors.

Now let's step back and revisit the question of what's in a name. Again, my answer is there is plenty in a name if it has to do with your health and humongous if it has to do with life-and-death situations.

What's in a name? This is a question I have continued to struggle with for the last seven years since I completed my dissertation on telehealth or telemedicine. The reason this question continues to boggle my mind is because this wonderful way of delivering care called telehealth or telemedicine or electronic health has not gained the traction it deserves for various reasons. For me, I believe the name is one of the reasons. Various literatures have called it various names with different explanations to justify whatever it is called.

TELEHEALTH, TELEMEDICINE OR ELECTRONIC HEALTH WHY THE NAME MATTERS

Many of my discussions will focus on what we should call this mode of health-care delivery in order to push it to the mainstream usage for health care and make it a household name. With all the explanation and attached names, the most important message is that we need to publicize the availability of this mode of health-care delivery. We need to use a layman's terminology that is easy to remember and affiliate with. We need to make the name user-friendly for the consumers first and the providers second. We have to create an emotional attachment that will drive the health-care consumers and the health-care providers to want to use this valuable system of health-care delivery that is cost-effective, an excellent form of health-care delivery system, and user-friendly. The name we call this method of health-care delivery could make or break the way this mode of care delivery is perceived and utilized.

The three names, telehealth or telemedicine or electronic health, are all referring to the same mode of health-care delivery. When I did my first research seven years ago, I used the terminology *telehealth* in the majority of my writing and research paper. The problem I encountered then was that most health-care professionals were not familiar with the terminology seven years ago. This raises the question, how do you expect a health-care giver to encourage patient participation in a system that they are not familiar with? It is asking for the impossible. The names telehealth or telemedicine or electronic health are all used in this book to make sure the health-care recipient and the health-care providers are all on the same level of understanding as regards to the names for the remote health-care delivery system in question. I am assuming that the providers might prefer using the name telehealth, or telemedicine, while the health-care consumers might use the name electronic health. I am advocating the emphasis of public awareness in the following areas:

PUBLIC AWARENESS OF THE AVAILABILITY OF ELECTRONIC HEALTH-CARE DELIVERY MODE

- Recognize that there is another mode of health-care delivery system that is different from the traditional face-to-face system as we know it today.
- Recognize that the name electronic health-care mode of care delivery is synonymous with the name telehealth or telemedicine mode of health-care delivery.
- Recognize that this mode of health-care delivery is being covered by most insurance companies, and the consumers should become educated consumers by asking their health-care providers about electronic mode of delivering health care.
- Consumers should try this mode of health-care delivery. It is by trying it out that the consumers will gain more knowledge and confidence about the advantages of electronic health.
- Consumers should spread the news of electronic health-care delivery by word of mouth. Word of mouth is the best form of advertisement.
- The consumers should become the champions who will market this wonderful mode of health-care delivery by giving personal testimonies.

The world of technology has created an opportunity that must not be missed. We live in a world where every age group, from newborn to the centenarian, is exposed to the world of technology either in a small scale or large scale. From simple cell phone to advanced videoconferencing, telehealth or telemedicine or electronic health is a doable mode of health-care delivery. We need to think like a business person. To be successful in business, you need to be customer friendly and deliver a user-friendly and customer-friendly product. We need to remember that when a product is for sale, no matter how good that product is, you will not be successful in selling it if no consumer will buy the product. For consumers to be aware of a product and buy it, you have to advertise the product. Seven years ago when I first conducted my research, the world was not as familiar with the words *telehealth, telemedicine,* or *electronic health* as they are today. Even seven years later, the name is still not as popular as it should be. This is one of the reasons I am advocating for this mode of health-care delivery. The following three measures would do wonders for electronic health if properly executed.

- Advertising by various media. Word of mouth and testimonies of current users would do wonders for this mode of health-care delivery. I completed a one-year certificate program at Hunter College in Manhattan in 2012/2013. During that time, we had various speakers from the telehealth or telemedicine or electronic health industries who came and did presentations and gave various speeches to the educators in our class. These speakers have so much information to give out, and yet a lot of the general public, educators, clinicians, and lay citizens who need to know these information are not in the loop. Completion of that program also rekindled my interest in getting the word out to the general public.

- Publishing the cost-effectiveness of this mode of health-care delivery. The second reason I am advocating for this mode of health-care delivery is the cost-effectiveness of this mode of health-care delivery. Every chief operating officer, president, and chief financial officer of any health-care organization knows that health-care management is not business as usual anymore. Health-care organizations are forced to be prudent in the way they manage their patients today. Days of wastes are over; cost-effectiveness and prudent care management and population management are the orders of the day. More so now than ever, cost-effectiveness is the fashion of the day, or the financial burdens will prove to be financial suicide for health-care companies not prudent in managing their patients. Even before Affordable Health Care Act, or Obama Care, telehealth or telemedicine or electronic health care was a proven way to deliver quality health care and save money at the same time. With the current world of Affordable Health Care, or Obama Care, it is a no-brainer to adopt telehealth or telemedicine or electronic health-care mode into practice. The cost-effectiveness and savings will be worth the investment.

- Consumer satisfaction. The third reason to adopt teleheath or telemedicine or electronic health mode of health-care delivery into practice is the consumer satisfaction part of the equation. We as health-care providers need to put back on our business hats. The cost of health-care delivery is very high, and quality of health care delivered does not match the cost. The same way we search for sale items without compromising quality in purchasing our day-to-day needs, so must we search for a better way of delivering health care at an affordable cost without compromising quality. Consumers these days are always rating their experiences via Facebook, Twitter, FaceTime, phone calls, e-mails, text messaging, Instagram, blogs, etc. These are all the same systems where telehealth or telemedicine or electronic health is delivered. It is a no-brainer that the consumers are going to have high satisfaction rating for this mode of health-care delivery, when properly and securely delivered, because they are already using most of these systems in their daily-life activities. It is a natural for them, and they are familiar with using these types of systems in their daily communication.

Adopting telehealth or telemedicine or electronic health and incorporating it nto managing the consumer's health care is seamless when properly coordinated.

Henceforth, for simplicity, we shall use the term telehealth for the rest of our discussion.

HEALTH-CARE RATINGS BY CONSUMERS AND THE GOVERNMENT

High satisfaction rating from health-care consumers is a must for survival in the health-care industry. Health-care agencies are rated on various performances, including consumer satisfaction. These ratings are public information, which are published on the Internet as noted below:

National Rankings for Home Health Agencies

Please select your state's initials and press the **Show Results** button.

Select your State by initial:

Show Results

Go to the website below for more information.

CMS.gov
Centers for Medicare & Medicaid Services (retrieved 11/10/2013)

We computed home health-care rankings using publicly reported data downloaded from the Centers for Medicare & Medicaid Services (CMS) Medicare website (**www.medicare.gov/Download/DownloadDB.asp**, last accessed 7/23/2013). Rates are based on episodes of care occurring between April 1, 2012, and March 31, 2013.

Quality Measures

Quality measures are standard ways of measuring quality in health care, be it in a hospital setting, nursing home, or home care setting. Each of these settings is held to a certain standard, and quality measures have the specified criteria with which the quality measures are based.

Let's use the home health quality measure as an example.

The home health-care quality is measured with the Home Health Compare data set. This data set contains agency-specific, risk-adjusted performance on twenty-two quality measures for over twelve thousand agencies nationwide.

The quality measures are based on the following performances:

- How often home care agencies gave recommended care based on research best practice and best result.
- How often patient improved in certain important areas of care.
- How often patient needed unplanned medical care or had to be admitted to the hospital.
- All twenty-two quality measures are used to analyze these results.
- CMS usually suppresses the results for smaller agencies in order to avoid skewing the results.
- How often patients got better at walking and moving around.
- How often patients got better at getting in and out of bed.
- How often patients got better at taking a bath.
- How often patients were assessed for pain (pain is considered the fifth vital sign).
- How often patients were treated for their pain.
- Reduction in hospitalization is often highlighted, and CMS penalizes agencies financially for frequent hospitalization, while rewarding agencies with less hospitalization.
- Ranking of agencies are based on averaging scores of each agency on the five ranking questions.
- Performance is then based on percentile.
- The twenty-five questions are condensed into three questions about care received and two global questions about satisfaction.
- The agencies are also ranked in percentiles. For example, an agency ranking 100th percentile does not mean the agency got 100 percent in the ranking; it just means they did better than all other agencies.
- The results are published on the HCAHPS website.

Mode of Survey Administration

These surveys are randomly sent out. Usually, a hard copy is sent to a cross section of patients with varied diagnosis.

The chosen patients are current patients in addition to those patients who were discharged within forty-eight hours to six weeks after receiving home care.

CMS.gov
Centers for Medicare & Medicaid Services (retrieved 11/10/2013)

Now let's get back to the question: What's in a name? Answer as you wish, but I say plenty if it has to do with your health and humongous if your life depends on it.

As the debate and chaos rages on in Washington and our nation over Obama Care, or Affordable Care Act (ACA), there are a lot of conversations that need to take place about telehealth. You choose the name you wish to call it, but call it a name that is meaningful to you. Call it a name that helps you remember that if your life depends on it, you must remember the name. If the life of the consumers or health-care recipients who are counting on you to help them make the right decision depends on it, you are giving them the information that they need to know. Calling the health care reform act Affordable Care Act brought less resistance for some rather than calling it Obama Care. The same principle will apply here. The beauty of it all is that there are three name choices to choose from. No need to worry. Choose a name to call it, but call it a name that helps you remember that there is another mode of receiving health care called telehealth mode of delivering care. Yes, it is a choice of health-care delivery that the public needs to be aware of, and it is a choice that the public should be encouraged to explore. Having choices enhances informed decision making, so it should be the same here. During a recent news poll of random citizens, the responses of some of the citizens polled were funny in the sense that it reflects the answer to the question "what's in a name?" Obama Care versus Affordable Care Act. Same program, different names. The response from those lacking understanding of the names was often, "No, Obama Care is not good. Affordable Care Act is good, just listen to the names."

THE FREEDOM AND EXPERIENCE OF KNOWING

Now let's assume that all the kinks and maladies involved with Affordable Care Act, or Obama Care, has been resolved and we all are at a level playing field of having access to health care and have understanding of what type of care we are entitled to, then what's next?

I would like the nation to remember a *name*, a name associated with health care, a name associated with accessible health care, a name associated with cost cutting, a name associated with easy access, a name that must be invoked for a successful and healthy nation, a name that must be pushed to the forefront in this fight for Affordable Health Care Act, a name that we as a nation should not allow to waste away in the back burner, a name that must be known by the world at large. That name is telehealth.

I remember my first experience with telehealth. I was in charge of a telemetry unit at one of the local hospitals, and it was an experience to be cherished because of the freedom it afforded the patients on this unit. The patients were connected to a small box that they wore in order to experience the freedom rarely afforded very ill hospitalized patients with a heart condition. This small but portable box, simply known as telemetry box, was the key to their freedom. These telemetry units were wired so that the nurses were able to monitor the patients via an electronic monitor at the nurses' station. The joy of freedom was often noted as the patients were not restricted to their beds. They were free to roam the unit while the nurses were able to monitor their condition from a distance. Even though the distance was within the confinement of the designated telemetry unit, it was still a welcome freedom enjoyed and appreciated by the patients. Most of these patients were coming from more restricted areas like the emergency room or the medical intensive care unit.

Notice that I used the word *freedom*. Yes, *freedom* is the key word here. If you know anything about mind and body connection, you would know that 50 percent of healing from most illnesses takes place in the mind. So to backtrack a little, the fact that these patients were free to walk around was a big deal to them. They were attached to these telemetry boxes that gave them the freedom to walk around with the confidence that there were health-care providers watching out for their health. This knowledge and confidence gained automatically helped to improve the health of these patients. Now let's backtrack one more time and apply the same principle to the use of telehealth. As much as the freedom of movement noted above is always greatly appreciated by the patients, now fast-forward to today and imagine what telehealth is able to do for your patients. The possibilities are unimaginable and unlimited, to say the least.

THE BENEFITS OF TELEHEALTH, TELEMEDICINE OR ELECTRONIC HEALTH TO CONSUMERS AND PROVIDERS

Utilization of telehealth provides the following benefits for the health-care recipients:

- Peace of mind that a health-care provider is monitoring their condition.
- Confidence that they have a health-care provider to work with.
- Can easily access a health-care provider without extensive traveling.
- Can save the cost of transportation to and from the health-care provider's office.
- Can save money on health care due to low cost of care for telehealth versus face-to-face visit. For example, no copay for electronic visits versus copay for face-to-face visits.
- For private payers, it is a low fee for telehealth visits versus face-to-face visits.
- Can avoid losing time from work due to minor illnesses. This automatically translates to more time or more money if the time saved can be cashed by the patient.
- Quicker access to health care due to ability of health-care providers to be more accessible.
- Ability to cater to more patients via telehealth.
- More relaxed encounter with health-care visits as compared to anxiety involved during face-to-face visits, etc.

Utilization of telehealth provides the following benefits for the health-care providers:

- Can easily provide care to the health-care recipients without extensive traveling.
- Can save cost of traveling that is often budgeted as part of providing care and reimbursed to staff on a weekly or monthly basis.
- Can save money on health-care overhead due to low cost of space, staffing, utilities, stationeries, securities, etc., for telehealth versus face-to-face visit.
- Will gain more business due to ability to provide high-quality care at low cost. For example, no copay for electronic visits versus copay for face-to-face visits.
- Will gain more private payers business for a low fee for telehealth visits versus face-to-face visits.
- Will gain more business from patients who wish to avoid losing time from work due to minor illnesses.
- Will gain more business from patients and contractors looking for quicker access to health care due to ability of health-care providers to be more accessible due to their ability to cater to more patients via telehealth.
- Will gain higher patient satisfaction survey results due to more relaxed encounters with health-care providers during visits as compared to anxiety involved during face-to-face visits, etc.

STEP-BY-STEP EXAMPLE OF A TELADOC VIDEO CONFERENCING VISIT

- The first step is to register as a customer and then log into your account or call their number, 1-800-Teladoc, to arrange an appointment.
- The second step is to talk to a doctor.
- The third step is to have your issues managed via video conversation. If prescription is needed, it will be sent to your local pharmacy electronically.
- The last step is you settle your bill, and you are done.

As per Teladoc website, the average wait time to see a doctor is twenty-four minutes. This is in contrast to approximately four hours of an emergency room wait time. When you subtract the travel time to and from the emergency room or doctor's office, you start to realize the value.

Telehealth or Telemedicine Simplified (a.k.a. Electronic

Health Simplified)

The name telehealth is so simple, or not so, depending on your audience. It also depends on the knowledge of your audience or their knowledge deficit.

Telehealth is a form of health-care delivery via use of electronic devices (nonvideo or video) to communicate and treat a health-care recipient located at a remote site.

Below is another definition of telehealth:

"Telehealth is defined as the use of medical information sent from one site to another through electronic communications to improve patients' healthcare. Telehealth is a rapidly developing approach of delivering medical care where medical information is transferred through interactive hardware and/or software media for the purpose of consulting, and performing remote medical procedures or examinations via remote site. Telemedicine includes a variety of medical programs and service types provided for the patient via remote site."

You wake up one morning with sudden cold-like symptoms: stuffy nose, cough, congestion. You have trouble getting an appointment with your existing doctor, and you don't want to miss time at work by sitting in an urgent care or ER waiting room. What to do?

Step 1

Contact Teladoc.

Simply log in to your account or call 1-800-Teladoc to request a phone or online video consult with a Teladoc doctor.

The average doctor call-back time is twenty-four minutes.

Step 2

Talk with a doctor.

A U.S. board-certified doctor or pediatrician licensed in your state reviews your Electronic Health Record (EHR), then contacts you, listens to your concerns and asks questions. It's just like an in-person consult.

There is no time limit to the consult.

Step 3

Resolve your issues.

The doctor recommends the right treatment for your medical issue. If a prescription is necessary, it's sent to the pharmacy of your choice.

Ninety percent of members report that the Teladoc doctor resolved their issue.

Step 4

Settle your bill.

Teladoc charges the credit card you provided when requesting your consult or your billing information on file. You can request a receipt for deductibles or reimbursement, if needed. The doctor updates your HIPAA-compliant EHR based upon the consult.

Teladoc is a qualified expense for HSA, FSA, and HRA accounts.

Step 5

Smile.

At the end of every call, the doctor will ask if he's answered all of your questions, and we'll follow up to make sure you're delighted with the service. With your permission, we can even send a record of your encounter to your current doctor.

Ninety-five percent of members were happy with their consult, and ninety-five percent said they'd use Teladoc again.

The Teladoc system allows health care recipients to transmit or communicate their symptoms, 24/7, from the convenience of their home, office, hotel or mountaintop (www.Teladoc.com).

What is a Teladoc? This is a telehealth provider.

"The nation's first and largest Tele-health provider with more than 6 million members announced today the acquisition of Consult A Doctor, a Tele-health company founded in 2007. With this acquisition, individuals and employees of small to medium sized businesses will now have access to Tela-doc's national network of U.S. board-certified, state licensed physician for consults" (Lockhart 2013).

Now what's in a name?

Telehealth can be defined as an electronic system of delivering and receiving health care via a remote access. For simplicity's sake, there are two main forms of this type of electronic care delivery system as noted below:

1. Plain old telephone and fax system
2. Videoconferencing system

The plain old fax and telephone system is the very old form of telehealth system. This has been going on since the phone was invented. Usually it was for the rich and famous until the phone became a tool used by the general public. As the technology evolved and the cell phones became smart phones and tools affordable to the lower class in both the developed and the third-world countries, telehealth became available to the general public, as long as a willing licensed health-care provider and a willing health-care recipient have mutual understanding and are partners in caring. Below are the mechanisms utilized in this mode of care delivery.

1. *Store and forward* (S&F) system of telehealth care involves a system where patients, caregivers, or significant others are able to self-monitor the affected health condition as instructed by the health-care givers. Usually, these are nonclinicians who are taught how to use the necessary equipment. For example, blood pressure machine, blood sugar equipment, weight scale, etc. The results are uploaded and transmitted into a system where the health-care giver retrieves the information as it is transmitted or at a specified time. The health-care giver analyzes the results and then calls the patient or health-care receiver on the phone to recommend treatment based on the health information sent via the store and forward system. The treatment could be a standing order that is preprescribed by the health-care giver. For example, a sliding scale insulin order prescribed based on the blood sugar level, a standing order for a water pill based on the patient's weight gain, etc.
2. *The videoconferencing* is the more sophisticated form of telehealth. This is a system of health-care delivery where the health-care deliverer and health-care recipient are able to see each other during the process of care or consultation. The patients at the receiving sites are receiving the same type of care that they would have received had they been face-to-face with the health-care provider. The videoconferencing is gaining momentum in a lot of health care and educational settings. This is a sure way of breaking boundaries. The health-care receivers and health-care deliverers are saved a lot of stress in traveling time. Both parties are saved a lot of money in

traveling costs. Our health-care system will be more cost-effective and more user-friendly as we warm up to this new and improved way of care delivery.

The adage "It's a small world after all" truly comes to play here when a specialist like a surgeon can perform surgery by operating via a robotic arm anywhere in the world.

Videoconferencing is used to educate patients, medical students, nursing students, and all other health professionals all over the world.

The videoconferencing affords just-in-time care to the recipient at a fraction of the cost it would have cost for a face-to-face encounter without the aid of telehealth.

As the world evolves to this age of smart phones, text messaging, Skype, videoconferencing, FaceTime, Instagram, etc., electronic health-care delivery is including all of the above in this rapidly evolving method of health-care delivery. The health-care industry is struggling to catch up as the technologically savvy health-care recipients are forging ahead and demanding care be delivered their way—the new technology way.

Newest Terminologies

- **Flipping**

This is the terminology used to describe the method of teaching students by using technology to download their lectures. It is reviewed before class so that class time is used for discussion rather than lecturing.

- **Techno-Tots**

The second newest terminology is *techno-tots*. This is the terminology used to describe the use of technology by children as young as infants. This is well depicted in the *Parent Today* magazine of April 2013 with a picture of an infant already using an iPad to connect with parents.

This is welcome news for electronic health advocates. Who better to embrace electronic health than a generation of tots who are raised from day one on use of iPads and other electronic gadgets? A survey has shown that approximately 37 percent of infants are playing with iPads. This news is one big advantage for the electronic health world.

The electronic-savvy patients of this electronic age can perform the following:

- E-mail their symptoms.
- Access some of their health information by signing on to their patient's portal based on the type of access provided by their physician.
- They can snap a picture of their injuries or skin condition and send it to their doctor via their cell phones.
- The patients can snap real-time pictures of their health condition as it is happening and send it to their health-care provider in real time.
- Patients can snap their real-time experience in a health-care setting and immediately critique their health-care experience in an online blog or Instagram.
- A video recording is even better as the patients are able to tell their stories in real time with a video to corroborate their experiences.

DELIVERING THE MESSAGE TO THE SOURCE FOR HIGH-IMPACT RESULTS

Care coordination with patient participation is extremely possible and highly effective with the two simplified representation of telehealth mode of health-care delivery outlined above.

The average patient is interested in participating in self-care. Evidence-based health-care practices have shown that the most successful and most effective programs in health care are those that seek input and participation from the individuals for whom the care is being designed.

Heavy hands-on by the clinicians is not always the best way to provide care, and this type of heavy hands-on care is becoming a thing of the past. Care coordination and customized package type of care is the order of the day.

Population management and the care coordination type of care model is a very user-friendly type of model in telehealth delivery system. The customization of certain types of disease management models of care makes it easy to standardize the way care is delivered. The health-care deliverers are able to quickly render care via a standardized or customized set of evidence-based care delivery model or standing order.

Health-care givers with a standing order are able to electronically deliver care timely and

- with evidence-based confidence and result,
- with patient and caregiver participation,
- with cost savings that is measurable in real time, and
- with high level of patient satisfaction.

Examples:

- Harlem prostate cancer screening: This was an evidence-based community program. It involved a mobile health-care system where the church, community, and barbershop partnered to provide health-care treatment and screening in the local community where the recipients live and frequent.
- This type of principle applies to the telehealth situation. You are giving health-care recipients the opportunity to receive care in their community with people they are familiar with and at an affordable cost.

>> www.hhs.gov

Teenage Pregnancy Prevention Program

This is another example of an effective program using electronic education and visits as needed. New York City Department of Health and Planned Parenthood coordinated their efforts to reduce teen pregnancy via various use of electronic education and care delivery. They were successful in achieving 30 percent reduction in teen pregnancy rate from 2011 to 2012. The program became a success due to easy access, electronic health-care usage, and community involvement, including the school community (NYC Teen, retrieved 11/2/2013).

This is a process that will help the telehealth to be successful by applying the same principle: bring care to consumers in their community. This process also enhances care provision in a comfortable environment with equipment and gadgets the consumers are familiar and comfortable with.

Obesity Prevention Program

This is another example of a successful program utilizing electronic health. The principle stays the same. The accessibility and ease of providing the educational information necessary for educating patients and caregivers made this program a success. Necessary information on obesity was made available electronically. This is a form of telehealth. The easy access and the availability of educational material on demand were helpful in educating the participants and attaining success in the obesity prevention program (American Academy of Pediatrics 10/1/2013).

Campaign to Spread Awareness on World Stroke Day

This is another example of spreading the word by using the right name, electronic messages, and best practice.

The *Times of India* (published on October 29, 2013) chronicled a story of how a team of health-care professionals from Gujarat, India, was able to successfully run a campaign to spread awareness of stroke prevention in India. The team made awareness a top priority in their chosen Indian territories of Waghodia, GIDC, Dabhoi, Asoi, Savli, Sokhada, Sankheda, Rameshara, Alkapuri, and Karelibaug. They involved the locals in this effort.

The planned activities included the following:

- They invited the community for firsthand marketing of their state-of-the-art neuroscience facility and comprehensive stroke unit that has set a benchmark in handling stroke.
- They held informational sessions for the community and family members of stroke victims.
- They used testimonies from patients and family members detailing their experiences of debilitation from stroke to functional state after treatment from the stroke center.
- Emphasis was laid on the point that swift action is key to recovery from the debilitation of stroke and its residual symptoms.

The ability to have firsthand information available via electronic health or face-to-face while pushing awareness is critical to success. This is also the period of pushing your key points and building trust. For stroke awareness, swift action was emphasized because when stroke happens, there are narrow windows of opportunity for maximum recovery if time is not wasted in seeking help. Once the consumers get the key message and trust is established, the consumers of health will become your allies in using word of mouth to spread the good news. This is one evidence-based way of spreading the good news of cost-effectiveness, good health care, and better time management for health-care delivery via telehealth (Prashant Rupera October 29, 2013, timesofindia.indiatimes.com).

The success of this project was based on the following:

- Aligning professionals.
- Having a theme for the campaign—"World Stroke Day." ("Electronic Health-Care Delivery Awareness Day" would also make a good theme for the campaign to publicize electronic health delivery.)
- Tapping into the knowledge base of the professionals and the locals.

- Involving the local people.
- Involving the local hospitals was also prominently mentioned.

This process is extremely important. As we push forward the campaign to increase the utilization of electronic health, we cannot negate the importance of collaboration with our local hospitals. In instances where there is a need to seek in-hospital care after consultation via electronic health, it is an added comfort for all parties to know that the hospitals are up-to-date with the available electronic health resources available in their community.

These added resources should add some comfort to the community hospitals, which used to get clogged-up emergency rooms due to patients whose signs and symptoms did not warrant an emergency room visit, but for lack of a place to turn to or lack of knowledge of available electronic health access, the patients had no choice but to head to the nearest hospital emergency room and clog up the system waiting to be seen. Most consumers do not realize that emergency rooms have a triage level or category system. You are often seen by your triage level, not by your time of arrival in the emergency room. Once this triage category system is explained and understood by the general public, the incentive to visit the emergency room with a minor complaint will definitely wane out.

What Is a Triage Category Level?

- Triage category level is a system of categorizing the severity of patients' complaints so that a physician can see them in a timely manner based on the severity of their illness before their condition starts to deteriorate.
- Triage level is usually categorized in three to five levels.

Level I type of patients. This is usually the sickest level. This could be as serious as a patient who has had a heart attack and is unconscious and requires chest compression in attempt to bring the patient back to life, or a patient who was involved in a serious car accident or has a gunshot wound to the heart and is not breathing well and not awake.

This type of state is considered an emergent state or critical and unstable state. The patient in this state is also considered in need of emergent care. This is one type of patient considered to be appropriate for level I trauma centers.

Level II type of patients. These are also very sick patients, but their condition could be considered critical but stable. These could be patients that are experiencing signs and symptoms of heart attack—chest pain, dizziness, diaphoresis, and unstable blood pressure, pulse, and breathing. These could also be patients who have a gunshot wound on the thigh, leg, or arm. These could also include those patients involved in not-so-serious motor vehicle accidents, such as leg and arm fractures, abdominal obstruction, appendicitis, etc. These types of patients need care in an emergency room for immediate treatment in order to avoid further damage and complication.

Level III type of patients. These are moderately sick patients who need attention within two to four hours, and the delay will not cause any further complication to their condition. These could be patients with abdominal pain, stomach virus, etc.

Level IV type of patients. These are patients whose care can wait for up to six to eight hours with no further complications to their condition. These could be patients with benign headache or pinkeye, patients requiring minor stitches, patients requiring suture removal, etc.

Level V type of patients. These are patients whose condition can be treated in a clinic setting or urgent care or telehealth type of system, like Teladoc. These are minor colds, allergies, aches, and pains, etc.

- Getting the word out by having the feet on the ground. This can be complemented by electronic education.
- Training the locals to act as the trainers.
- Showcasing the results of the efforts of the campaign.

Breast Cancer Initiative: An Evidence-Based Example

This is an example of how to roll out a program or project. The breast cancer initiative was a program conducted at NYU Cancer Institute in New York City. The NYU Cancer Institute offered a group of patient-individualized services. These services were personalized informative care with unique effective treatment options. There were multidisciplinary teams of specialists. These specialists consisted of medical oncologists, surgery team, radiation therapists, radiologists, and pathologists. These teams of specialists met weekly to discuss an individual condition and lifestyle needs, and then created a personalized cancer care plan.

Women with breast cancer are said to receive outpatient care at the NYU clinic, Thirty-Fourth Street in Manhattan. It is reported that this clinic centralizes all innovative, state-of-the-art care. This innovative care encompasses screening, diagnosis, treatment, genetic counseling, and supportive care in one pleasant and comfortable location.

This clinic serves as a multidiscipline, multicultural center of innovative care all housed in Manhattan. This is a microcosm of what effective and innovative care should be. The multidisciplinary team researches the challenges to care encountered by these groups of patients and their team, and then it formulates solutions to resolve the challenges. Some of their research is focused on the following:

- Increasing the number of minority and the underserved population.
- Understanding how certain hormones affect the development and spread of cancer.
- How breast cancer spreads and invades other body structures.
- Breast cancer immunity and how breast tumors are able to evade the immune system.
- Effects of radiation treatment on breast tissues and how to deliver safe and effective radiation to breast tissues.
- Identification of certain types of genes associated with an increased risk of breast cancer.

This type of model of care can be replicated in an environment where electronic health is being utilized. Using the theme of population management, the electronic health utilization can be customized to a specific population based on information derived from the use of electronic health usage. Once customized, the information could be used to enhance and upgrade the current usage, thereby optimizing the usage and making it more cost-effective and user-friendly (mednyu. edu).

As noted in the cited studies above, the health-care delivery made a difference in how the patients or health-care recipients responded to the care delivered to them. Mostly positive because it was tailored to their individual needs. Health-care delivery is not just about delivery care; it is also about the following:

- **Type of care delivered.**
- **The mode of delivering the care.**
- **Understanding the culture of the care recipients and leveraging that in the care delivery process.**
- Using evidence-based practice to provide appropriate care.
- Understanding on the part of the audience that care is being provided for, and using the appropriate mode of care delivery that will appeal to them.
- Being flexible to accommodate the demand of the audience to which the care is tailored, while staying within the confinement of the rules and regulations governing our practice.

As we as a nation take a critical look at our care delivery system and plan to reinvent it, we need to take a critical look at the above examples and others like it. We need to put our boots on the ground and leverage what we already have in our local and global community.

We need not reinvent the wheel.

At the end of the day, what matters the most is that we provide quality, cost-effective care to satisfied consumers. To this effect, we must be creative within the rules and regulations governing our practice in order to help us achieve the needed results.

PATIENT BILL OF RIGHTS AND RESPONSIBILITIES

As we continue to advocate for efficient, cost-effective, user-friendly mode of care delivery, we also need to remember to abide by the Patient Bill of Rights governing the care we provide as dictated by our various states and institution. Below is a generic summary of the Patient Bill of Rights and Responsibilities that could be customized by any health-care institution or health-care agency:

Most health-care institutions seek to provide exceptional care and provide the best possible experience for every patient and family. By making sure that patients and caregivers understand their rights and responsibilities, most of the above-stated goals are usually achieved.

Below are generic terms that are customized by various health-care settings in drafting their Patient Bill of Rights.

- You the patient is expected to be treated with dignity and respect.
- Your psychosocial, spiritual, and cultural beliefs are to be respected.
- You have the right to be comfortable and safe.
- You have the right to be treated with respect and dignity; in so doing, you will be provided with dignified care regardless of your color, race, religion, or sexual preferences, gender, national origin, language needs, disability, handicap, age, or any other status protected by relevant law.
- You have the right to practice your spiritual and cultural belief preferences as long as it does not interfere with the care of others or your treatment plan.
- You have the right to request and obtain the below information from your health-care team:

  o Your diagnosis, treatment, and prognosis in terms you can understand.
  o Your role in your care.
  o Treatment options.
  o Expected course of the treatment and/or recovery.
  o Benefits and risks of treatments.

o   The names of the physicians responsible for your care.

o   Any proposed clinical trials affecting your care or treatment.

You have the right to refuse to participate in such trials. If you refuse, you have the right to know that your refusal will not affect your access to continued care.

- You have the right to know that medical evaluation, treatment, and referral services are available at various health-care settings; to this effect, referral services can be made on your behalf as needed. If one institution is not able to meet your needs or if you request a transfer, the institution is obligated to facilitate your request for transfer to another health-care institution or health-care agency without fear of punishment or harassment after explaining the following to you:

o   You receive information about why the transfer is needed.

o   You receive information about the options available to you in lieu of a transfer.

o   You receive confirmation that communication has been established with the receiving institution or agency, and they have agreed to the transfer.

- You have the right to appropriate continuity of care and referral services, i.e., notification of your physician that you are receiving medical care.
- You have the right to be referred for continuity of care as needed or as determined by your medical condition, including referral for follow-up appointments or discharge to the next step of care in your recovery process.
- You have the right to foreign language or sign language interpretation so that you are able to receive the care and information you need to participate in your care.
- You have the right to know the relationship of your health-care provider and staff with other health-care and educational institutions as it relates to your care.
- You have the right to be informed of any clinical trials as it relates to your care; you also have the right to be informed that your refusal to participate in these clinical trials will not result in any penalties as regards to the care you will receive.
- You have the right to receive calls from your family, spouse, significant others, domestic partners, children, etc.
- You have the right to request a copy of your medical record upon discharge.

- You also have the right to refuse visitors or phone calls at any time by informing the appropriate personnel about your intent.
- You have the right to receive a copy of the Patient's Bill of Rights. Most health-care institutions and health-care agencies will include this in your admission package upon admission to their institution or agency.
- You have the right to legally designate a representative to advocate/oversee your health-care needs.
- You or your health-care representative have the right to make decisions about your health-care needs.
- You and your health-care representative have the right to expect the following information:

  o   Information needed to give consent for proposed procedures.
  o   Information needed to give consent for treatment options.
  o   Information needed for advanced directives.
  o   Information needed in preparing living will or power of health care attorney—these are needed in case you become unable to make health-care decisions.

- You have the right to be informed that health-care institutions have ethic committees that can help you, your family, and your health-care team explore various health-care options and come to a decision about your health-care needs.
- You have the right to receive appropriate pain assessment and appropriate pain management—pain is currently designated as the fifth vital sign.
- You have the right to a safe health-care setting, free from verbal and physical abuse.
- You have the right to be free from physical and medical restrain, unless, it is needed for your safety and safety of the medical team.
- You have the right to comfort and dignity. If you are terminally ill, you have the right to have your symptoms treated, your pain managed, and have your family and caregiver receive the support they need to address psychosocial and spiritual concerns related to your terminal condition.
- You have the right to privacy and confidentiality about your medical and mental condition. Discussions, consultations, examinations, and your treatments should be conducted discreetly.
- You have the right to have your care provided in a setting that provides as much privacy as possible. Those not directly involved in your care must have your permission to be present.
- You have the right to choose where you receive care. This includes the freedom of receiving care from a place of comfort—could be your home via telehealth.

- You have the right to save money while receiving care in terms of not spending money on transportation to make a doctor visit—telehealth visit will take care of this.
- You have the right to decide your choice of how you receive health care—telehealth is included.
- You have the right to refuse contact with health-care staff not involved with your care.
- You have the right to request the presence of members of your own gender upon request during examination or procedures performed by a health-care professional of opposite gender.
- You have the right to receive and examine and seek explanation of your bill regardless of the source of payment.

Other rights and responsibilities may also exist depending on the state, institution, or agency providing care.

❖ Patient Responsibilities

Just as much as we have held our health-care institutions and health-care agencies responsible for a lot of the Patient Bill of Rights and Responsibilities, patients are also held responsible for certain aspects of the care they receive in our institutions or health-care agencies.

Most health-care institutions and agencies expect a certain level of cooperation and transparency from patients and caregivers in order to be able to provide the care needed and able to afford the patients and families a high-quality, accurate treatment and decent care. The patient is responsible for the following:

✓ Provide accurate and complete information about your health to the best of your knowledge. These information should include, but not limited to, the following:

   o   Nature of your illness, including your signs and symptoms
   o   All specific signs and symptoms relating to your current conditions
   o   All past medical histories
   o   All past hospitalizations
   o   Medication histories
   o   Medication and food allergies
   o   Changes in your medical conditions as they occur
   o   Any advanced directives you have prepared

- Ask questions and expect to get answers regarding your medical plan and your expected roles in accomplishing your medical plan.
- You are expected to make informed decisions about your medical plan, so ask questions to help you clarify any doubts.
- You are expected to participate in the medical plan as put together by you and your medical team.
- You have the right to refuse treatment at any time despite your knowledge of the consequences of your refusal.
- You are expected to follow hospital rules as they affect patient care; for example, you are expected to respect hospital properties, staff properties, and the properties of the other patients.
- Assist the health-care institutions to limit noise in their health-care settings.
- Assist the health-care institutions' effort to limit the number of visitors for safety and noise control purposes.
- Assist the health-care institutions in their effort to provide and comply with a smoke-free environment.
- Comply with health-care institutions' quest to create a health-care environment that is free of alcohol, tobacco products, weapons, illegal drugs, and all illegal items. In an effort to create a safe environment for their patients, health-care institutions have the right to authorize their designated staff or security departments to search patients' rooms or belongings for illegal items whenever there is a reason to suspect that such an item exists. You will be notified whenever possible and necessary that such a search will take place.
- You are responsible for providing accurate and timely information regarding source of payment for care rendered. You have the right to receive emergency treatment without delay.
- You are responsible for fulfilling your financial obligation for all the health-care treatments that you received.

Patient Population Management

Population management is a process of managing a group of patients with similar disease who require similar care. These groups of patients are identified as a population of certain groups who require certain/similar treatment. Via telehealth or electronic health, these groups of patients are managed in a similar way. The standard of care is preset and predictable.

Population management helps you to take advantage of scarce resources and lower the cost of care.

athenahealth is one of the many population management companies out there helping the health-care industry be more efficient in the way health care is delivered by introducing the concept of population management. Below is a summary of the services they provide:

- Athenahealth delivers cloud-based services for EHR, practice management, and care coordination.
- EHR improves productivity and makes it easy to meet pay-for-performance measures.
- Cloud-based medical billing boosts medical billing on average of 8 percent.
- Physicians and patients can connect beyond the exam room with Athena communication featuring live and automated Athena communication services that reduces no-show by 8 percent.
- Athena coordinators streamline the coordination process to benefit the entire community. Service can improve revenue and physician loyalty and facilitate a red-carpet experience for patients (http://www.athenahealth.com)

TELEHEALTH OR TELEMEDICINE OR ELECTRONIC HEALTH HINDRANCE TO GROWTH

As much as we advocate for increased use in telehealth, there are some issues and concerns that cause hindrance to the use of telehealth. Some of the issues hindering growth or general use of telehealth are listed below:

- Legal issues
- Financial reasons
- Confidentiality concerns
- Lack of infrastructure support
- Lack of support from the government and health-care community
- Lack of awareness by health-care providers
- Lack of awareness by health-care consumers

Benefits of Using Telehealth

Top Ten Reasons to Use Telehealth

1. It helps reduce hospital readmissions.
2. It improves clinical outcomes.
3. It helps decrease long-term health-care costs.
4. It improves patient's quality of life and longevity.
5. It improves patient's education, knowledge deficit, and self-care.
6. It improves patient's compliance to prescribed treatment.
7. It decreases frequency of ER visits.
8. It streamlines clinical workflow.
9. It catches early signs of decompensation.
10. It reduces the risk of patient mortality.

(Philips Electronics, retrieved July, 2013)

Funding

T here are grant programs that offer aid telehealth projects, as noted below:

Public Sources

o   The US Department of Health and Human Services (HRSA) provides a telehealth grantee directory (visit www.hrsa.gov) that includes a listing of all the grant programs available for telehealth projects. It is important to be aware that submission windows can be very short.

o   The World Health Organization (WHO) has put in place a report on e-Health tools and services that outline the needs and funding that will enable developing countries to utilize telehealth technologies. Visit www. who.org.

Private Sources

o   *The AT&T Foundation* has used its Excelerator Grant Program to advance telehealth. In 2006, the foundation awarded Oklahoma State University Center for Health Science (OSU-CHS) a grant for extending the school's growing network of telehealth sites in Eastern Oklahoma (http://www.healthsciences.okstate.edu/communications/ press_release/2006/2006_02_01_ATT.cfm). To learn more about AT&T Excelerator Awards Program, go to http://www.att.com/gen/ corporate-citizenship?pid=7745.

o   *HELP International Telemedicine Humanitarian Emergency Mobile Medical Clinic Network* is a telehealth-based online community of physicians, financial donors, and emergency personnel bringing advanced medical assistance to disaster zones and areas of chronic humanitarian need around the world. (http://www.netsquared.org/telehealth).

o   *International Health Group* at the University of Washington, promoting long-term careers in the service of disadvantaged populations worldwide through educational activities and the development of international research and clinical opportunities, has compiled a list of private funding sources for medical research projects (http://www.uwmedicine.org)

A general Internet search can provide several additional organizations that provide grant funding for starting telehealth programs.

Educational Leadership in Telehealth

AMD Global Telemedicine Inc. conducted an informal Internet search of US colleges and universities seeking any kind of telehealth initiatives offered. According to AMD Global Telemedicine researcher Lara Saba, within US colleges and universities found on the Internet, only 14.6 percent offer telehealth courses, and only 7 percent of those same US. colleges and universities include telehealth clinics, centers, programs, institutes, etc.

Some schools within that 14.6 percent that have developed courses on telehealth include the following:

- Brody School of Medicine, East Carolina University (http://www.ecu.edu)
- University of Oklahoma (http://www.oubc.ou.edu)
- University of Vermont (http://www.med.uvm.edu)
- University of California-Davis (http://www.ucdavis.edu/spotlight/0407/telemedicine.html)
- Mount Aloysius College—offers a telehealth nursing course (http://www.mtaloy.edu/telehealth/)
- Nelda C. Stark College of Nursing and Center for Telenursing and Health Informatics at Texas Woman's University (https://www.twu.edu/nursing/default.asp)

For additional schools that offer telehealth courses, go to http://www.amdtelemedicine.com/links.cfm.

Additional online telehealth educational resources include:

- *AMD Global Telemedicine* (www.amdtelemedicine.com) offers both on-site installation and training, teleconferencing product demonstrations, or video training for telehealth devices and how to properly use these devices during telehealth encounters.
- *American Telemedicine Association (ATA)* (www.atmeda.org) has twelve special interest groups (business and finance, emergency preparedness and response, home telehealth and remote monitoring, human factors, international, ocular telehealth, technology, teledermatology, telemental health, telehealth nursing, telepathology, and telerehabilitation). The ATA is the leading organization for disseminating information and knowledge on telehealth. (ATA provides annual and midyear meetings addressing specialty areas of telehealth.)
- *Canadian Society of Telehealth (CST)* (www.cst-sct.org) features multiple programs, including podcasts that provide web-based telehealth programs, as well as an annual conference.

- *International Council of Nurses (ICN)* (www.icn.ch) has an online section on telenursing with both national and international resources.
- *International Society for Telemedicine and e-Health (ISfTeH)* (www.Isft.net) offers annual meetings, education, telehealth directory, and newsletters for members.
- *ITelehealth Inc.* (www.itelehealthinc.com) offers telehealth-educational presentations and products, as well as consulting services for nurses.
- *Med-e-Tel* (www.medetel.lu) is an annual exhibition and congress meeting that provides services, communications, education, and networking opportunities for health-care providers.

Telemedicine or Telehealth Today and Tomorrow

Telehealth applications extend the skills and knowledge nurses use every day. It is also one of the most promising and practical solutions available not only to address an inevitable nursing crisis but also to bring modern-day health care to more people and save more lives both in the United States and around the world.

Now it is a matter of mastering the tools and knowledge necessary to utilize this innovative process. Today's nurses should seize the opportunity and run with it (Castelli, Diane, RN, MS, MSN, retrieved 10/1/2013).

➤ Licensure Issues

Due to increased use of technology in our daily activities and the global use of electronic gadgets, the geographic boundary's restrictions have been shattered. This shattered boundary has created a fertile ground for increased access to health information and a robust opportunity for practice of telehealth across states' boundaries and international borders. Despite rapid growth in technology and the affordable electronic equipment that has made telehealth a more cost-effective mode of health-care delivery, the licensure issue continues to be a sticky point for health-care professionals. Licensure in the United States is embedded in a state-based licensure system. This state-based licensure system imposes limits on the expansion of the practice of telehealth or telemedicine or electronic health system. The current system of medical licensure is based on statutes written at the turn of the twentieth century, when it was never envisioned how electronic communication would impact our world like it has done today.

As we are now aware of the explosion of the electronic age and the influence it is already having on our health-care delivery system and the influence it will continue to have on our health-care delivery system in the near future and beyond, it is high time we revisit our licensure laws and redesign a new regulatory structure for the twenty-first century. There are proposals for national telehealth or telepharmacy licensure with the primary goal of developing a policy that will make national licensure possible. Once achieved, the national licensure will expand the telehealth market. It will also help to eliminate some of the regulatory and legal issues surrounding the telehealth mode of health-care delivery.

Telehealth has branched off to many specialties. There are as many specialties in telehealth as there are in the field of health care. The following are a few of the specialties in telehealth: telenursing, teleradiology, telesurgery, teledermatology, telementoring, telepsychiatry, telepsychotherapy, teleophthalmology, teledentistry, tele-ICU, etc. The list goes on.

Each of these specialties has the ability to practice across state lines and across international borders without leaving their local regions. There are certain limitations as different states are starting to regulate the practice of telehealth. Different organizations, including Joint Commission on Accreditation of Healthcare Organization (JCAHO) and National League for Nursing (NLN), are spearheading the reform process. The following are recent initiatives by various states, JCAHO, and National League for Nursing in the bid to regulate the practice of telehealth. The United States is a country that requires health-care professionals to be licensed in the state where they practice. This has created barriers in the practice of telehealth and is one of the reasons for the slow progress in the practice of telehealth in the United States. This barrier is handled differently by different specialties. Some specialties advocate for national certification, whereby each specialty will take a national exam, and once passed, the individual will be registered with a national registry and will be trackable in the national system. The Pharmacist Association is a strong advocate for national certification. This is the first attempt to deal with the licensing issues. This kind of system will allow the individual the freedom to practice nationally without having to travel to each state to seek licensure or registration to practice.

Pharmacy gross margins are declining at a rate of 4.5 percent each year.

- Medicare Part D reimbursements are declining, and pharmacies cannot keep up.
- Pharmacy management software allows a remote pharmacy to be established in underserved communities where a regular pharmacy was not economically viable. It also helps pharmacies that are busy to manage their workload.

"Tele-pharmacies' error rate is less than 1 percent, a 50 percent improvement over traditional practice and half the national average" (US Department of Health and Human Services).

For a successful implementation of a telehealth program,

- learn how to use the telehealth medical devices, as well as audio, video, and digital software applications over phone, integrated services digital network (ISDN), or internet provider (IP) communication networks;
- become techno-savvy in using other software applications for entering patient demographic data, saving, sending, and retrieving information to or from the consulting physician or nurse practitioner;
- collaborate with information technology staff, biomedical engineers, and telehealth physicians and nurses in one's health-care system or hospital as a telehealth or e-health team;
- assist in the development of telehealth guidelines, policies, and procedures;
- review and understand the applicable Health Insurance Portability and Accountability Act (HIPAA) laws with use of telehealth applications; and
- learn the evolution of telehealth or e-health technologies and how they are being used in health care.

Resources

Nurses can educate themselves on these areas in several ways, including the following:

- Seeking out telehealth information online.

  o American Telemedicine Association
  o Canadian Society of Telehealth
  o International Council of Nurses offers international competencies for telenursing
  o International Society for Telemedicine and e-Health
  o Telemedicine Information Exchange

- Attending telehealth conferences.

The proposal for national telehealth licensure is not yet approved. Consequently, practitioners are traveling to the states where they wish to practice and are obtaining multiple licensures in order to gain the privilege to practice telehealth. Countries like Canada, where their professionals are licensed by province, do not have this barrier. They have more leeway to practice telehealth.

The medical society and the nursing society are toiling with this licensing issue and yet have not reached a consensus on the final word about licensure. The

Federation of State Medical Boards (FSMB) proposed an act called the Model Act. This is the second attempt to deal with the licensing issue. The Model Act is a proposal that would allow a professional licensed in one state to apply for a limited license to practice telehealth in another state without having to seek licensure in the state that the professional wishes to practice at. The model act was proposed in order to help regulate the practice of telehealth across state borders. This proposal would allow a professional licensed in one state to apply for limited license to practice in another state. The third attempt to deal with the licensing issue was the introduction of the legislature that is titled Interstate Nursing Licensure Compact. This legislation was first proposed in 1997 by NSBN. This nurse compact legislature allows a nurse to have one license in his or her state of residency and to practice physically and electronically in other states subject to each state's practice law and regulation. Under the Interstate Nursing Licensure Compact, each state must achieve mutual recognition. This is done by enacting legislation authorizing the Nurse Licensure Compact. States enacting the compact also adopt administrative rules and regulations for implementation of the Compact. Each compact state must also designate a nurse licensure compact administrator whose job it is to facilitate the exchange of information between the states regarding compact nurse licensure and regulation. Nurse Licensure Compact Administrator (NLCA) was organized on January 10, 2000, to help protect the public health and safety by promoting compliance with the law. RNs and LPNs/LVNs have been included in the compact since 1998. Advanced practice nurses were recently included on August 16, 2002. Only the states that already have licensure compact have been allowed to adopt the Advanced Practice Compact. Utah was the first state to enact the Advanced Practice Compact on March 15, 2004 (NCSBN, Nurse Licensure Compact 2004).

Licensure of health-care professionals is currently a state-based system. Thus the practice of telehealth raises concerns regarding licensure and professional accountability, particularly relating to cross-state practice. In addition, the lack of reimbursement for telehealth services is seen as a barrier to the expansion of this practice.

Secondly, there is concern about state licensing of health practitioners who deliver services across state geographic boundaries. Recently, the Western Governors' Association called for a uniform state code for telehealth licensure and credentialing, which would define telehealth simplify licensure, and address continuing medical education. The Federation of State Medical Boards has been studying issues related to practice across state lines since 1994. In 1996, the federation proposed a limited license for use only in practicing medicine via electronic means across state boundaries. The American Medical Association opposed this concept. The National Council of State Boards of Nursing (NCSBN) has been developing a regulatory model that incorporates the characteristics of a multistate license. Such a license would be recognized nationally but enforced locally. NCSBN is expected to present this model in August at their annual meeting. Other groups, such as the Council of Licensure, Enforcement, and Regulation and the Interprofessional Workgroup on Health Professions, are also studying this issue. The federal government has also begun to take a serious look at telehealth. The Telecommunications Reform Act of 1996 charged the Department of Commerce and the Department of Health and Human Services and other appropriate agencies to submit a report analyzing telecommunications and its potential effects on the medical community. As a result, the Joint Working Group on Telemedicine (JWGT) was created. In the report, various licensure models that may be employed by the states were outlined. These approaches include the following: consulting exceptions, endorsement mutual recognition, reciprocity registration, limited licensure and national licensure.

The consulting exceptions model. This model allows out-of-state practitioners to practice in a state without obtaining licensure for the sole purpose of consulting. Most of these exceptions prohibit the unlicensed practitioner from opening an office or receiving phone calls within the state.

The endorsement model. This model allows state licensing boards to issue licenses to health professionals licensed in other states that have equivalent licensing standards.

The mutual recognition model. This model allows the licensing agencies in the participating states to voluntarily enter into an agreement to accept the policies and processes of licensure of a licensee's home state. This is the model currently being used throughout the European community and Australia.

The registration model. This model would allow out-of-state practitioners to inform the appropriate authorities that they would like to practice in the state on a part-time basis. This model would hold the out-of-state practitioners accountable for any misconduct occurring in the state where they are registered. The limited licensure model would limit the scope of practice rather than the period that an out-of-state practitioner may have within the state. Lastly, the national licensure model would require that a licensure system be implemented on the national level, thus disbanding the requirement for licensure in every state.

TELEHEALTH ADVANCEMENT ACT

Telehealth Advancement Act of 2011/2012 Law

Telehealth Advancement Act of 2011, which became a law in 2012, is one of Califonia's latest telehealth updates. The Telehealth Advancement Act became a law on January 1, 2012, as championed by Assemblyman Dan Logue, R-Lake Wildwood, and sponsored by California State Health Association. California has shown great courage and understanding of the benefits of telehealth. By passing the Advancement Act into law, California is able to remove policy barriers to telehealth use. Some of such barriers are noted below:

AB 415—This act updated the legal definition of telehealth to be more inclusive, made recommendations based on the experience of working with Center for Connected Health Policy (CCHP's telehealth model status report), recommended modernization of telehealth equipment and health force, streamlined the process of medical approval to be less burdensome, broadened types of services provided via telehealth, allowed all licensed health-care providers to engage in telehealth. It was documented that all these were done via overwhelming bipartisan support, with the following four democratic supporters: Wesley Chesbro (D-North Coast), Cathleen Galgiani (D-Livingston), Richard Pan (D-Natomas), and V. Manuel Pérez (D-Coachella).

AB 415 creates a level playing field among clinical services, regardless of whether they are delivered in person or via telehealth.

Telehealth, the new legal terminology, is defined as technology-enabled delivery of services rather than a specific medical practice. This broad terminology or definition allows for a far broader range of telehealth services than the old law and does not limit future telehealth technologies. This is so because it's encompassing and forward-looking by definition.

AB 415 did not make it mandatory for any institution or health-care agency to use telehealth. Institutions and agencies are free to review the facts and benefits and make up their mind as to implementing or not implementing telehealth.

Listed below are highlights of what Telehealth Advancement Act AB 415 does:

⬇ AB 415, signed into law in 2012, was able to update the use of the terminology *telemedicine* into *telehealth*. This upgrade allowed for more inclusive usage of telehealth by all health-care professionals instead of focusing on mainly the medical professionals when the term telemedicine was used. It also helped to broaden the usage of the system for all health care-related services and not just the medical part of health care. With this new law, other services included and covered are store and forward services, management of chronic diseases—such as blood pressure monitoring, blood sugar monitoring, weight monitoring for patients with congestive heart failure—medical data communications, high speed communications, and high definition communications that are e-mailed with attachments. This new law also covers transmission of photos, x-rays, videos, etc.

There are several studies to have shown that telehealth monitoring helps keep patients healthy, allows elderly and disabled patients to live at home and avoid having to move into skilled nursing facilities, and reduce hospitalizations and lengths of stay—all of which helps improve quality of life for patients and contain costs.

⬇ Another highlight of the Telehealth Advancement Act (AB 415) is that it eliminated the boundary issue. Under the old law, telehealth appointments had to take place only in licensed health-care facilities, such as hospitals or physician offices. The new law has no restriction as to where the appointment takes place as long as the HIPAA law and all privacy laws are followed. The health-care institutions and health-care agencies have to set their requirements. To this effect, the advice to these institutions and agencies is to seek counsel advice and use common sense in setting their requirements. The policy should not be so strict that it makes the system difficult to use and makes it not user-friendly to the customers, nor should it be so lax that it breaks HIPAA and privacy laws.

⬇ Another highlight of the Telehealth Advancement Act (AB 415) is that it eliminated the ban on use of e-mail and phone communications as part of telehealth services. This lift helped to expand the reach and payment for telehealth services. This lift is a real boost for companies that do care management for chronic medical conditions because they communicate their information mostly via e-mails and phone. There is no mandate to use e-mail or phone in telehealth communication, but it offers a great peace of mind to know that if a decision is made to use e-mail or phone, the cost will be covered.

This allows for substantial expansion of telehealth services. For example, disease management programs often include e-mail or telephone communications between patients and health professionals to ensure that patients are complying with treatment regimens and to check up on patients whose home monitoring programs have flagged a problem.

Studies have shown that disease management programs help keep patients healthy, help keep elderly and disabled patients out of skilled nursing facilities, and reduce both the number of hospitalizations and lengths of stay—all of which helps improve patients' quality of life and contains costs.

The next highlight is the inclusion of all health-care professionals licensed in California. This part of Telehealth Advancement Act (AB 415) is music to the ears of all health-care providers and recipients. This law makes it cost-effective for all health-care providers to provide appropriate care to all patients, with appropriate level staff, without overusing higher-skilled staff for lower-skill duties and vice versa.

Under the old law, only those designated as medical professionals, such as noted below, are allowed to practice as medical professionals that could provide telehealth services:

- Physicians
- Podiatrists
- Surgeons
- Clinical psychologists
- Marriage, family, and child counselors
- Dentists
- Ophthalmologists
- Optometrists (in limited scope)

The Telehealth Advancement Act provided an all-inclusive list of all California-licensed professionals. Below are some of the listed professionals:

- Registered nurses
- Physicians
- Pharmacists
- Nurse practitioners
- Physician assistants

- Dental hygienists
- Physical therapists
- Occupational therapists
- Speech and language pathologists
- Audiologists
- Licensed vocational nurses
- Psychologists
- Osteopaths
- Naturopaths

Telehealth Advancement law of 2012 (AB 415) allows California hospitals to use the new federal rules to make it easy to establish medical credentials for telehealth providers. The Telehealth Advancement Act of 2012 (AB 415) helps to clear the confusion of establishing streamlined processes so that telehealth medical credentialing is not caught up in a bottleneck process. This is possible because of the federal regulation called *privileging by proxy*. This is the process of allowing hospitals and other entities engaged in telehealth to accept the credentialing paperwork of each facility's practitioners. This makes for quicker approvals of practitioners and eliminates duplicative, expensive, and often cumbersome credentialing processes.

There is a new CMS rule that is also making telehealth user-friendly. This new CMS process also allows sites other than hospitals that engage in telehealth, such as physician offices and ambulatory centers, to use the same privileging by proxy processes for telehealth service delivered at hospitals. This process stands true as long as those services meet the hospital's conditions of practice.

One of the most important advantages of the Telehealth Advancement Act (AB 415) is the fact that Telehealth Amendment AB 415 aligns California law with the new CMS regulations. The confusion among California regulators centered on whether existing state regulations were in conflict with the new rule, and whether the state's hospitals would still have to go through full credentialing processes for all telehealth practitioners was immediately alleviated.

- Another highlight of the Telehealth Advancement Act 2012 law (AB 415) is the elimination of Medi-Cal's rule of asking health-care providers to document barriers to an in-person visit before a telehealth visit is authorized. This requirement was a great barrier to provision of telehealth to patients.
- Another highlight of the 2012 Telehealth Advancement law is the removal of the California sunset date for Medi-Cal coverage for store and forward for teledermatology, teleophthalmology, and teleoptometry.

⫩ The next highlight is the removal of request for additional written consent for telehealth. Verbal consent is deemed appropriate by the 2012 Telehealth Amendment Act law (cchpca.org/Tele-health-advancement-act, retrieved 9/25/2013).

Regulatory issues are discussed and decided at various levels. One of the best sites to obtain the latest and up to date information as regards to the latest legislation tracking is the American Telemedicine Association website as noted below:

http://www.americantelemed.org/docs/default-source/policy/state-telemedicine-legislation-matrix.pdf

Legal Issues

"Health care professionals increasingly face legal issues about the use of telecommunications, collectively known as 'Tele-health'" (Ziel 2004).

To date, there has been no reported legal issue related to the use of telehealth. Use of text messages, e-mails, and videoconferencing to communicate with physicians.

Use of these forms of communications are becoming commonplace. Medical insurance companies are also beginning to issue malpractice insurance on telehealth to health-care providers as noted below:

Telemedicine Medical Malpractice Insurance

Can You Insure Telemedicine?

Despite all the concerns and debate about the legal issues surrounding telehealth, there is no evidence of higher incidences of lawsuits due to use of telehealth. Most of the time, the topic focuses on the benefits of telehealth. Below are some of the benefits of telehealth:

o   Extended reach of specialty care in a more economical manner
o   Enhanced primary care services
o   Increased access to medical education and training programs in rural and underserved communities

Many physicians are informally engaged in telehealth. It is not uncommon these days for physicians and patients or parents of young children to engage in casual, unofficial exchange of medical information, such as exchanging pictures of rashes, bite or puncture wounds, or swollen or deformed fingers or other joints, etc. All the above-mentioned processes can be legal exchanges, which can be accomplished via secure site and be legally billed for via telehealth. Medical malpractice insurance's successful defense of a case is usually dependent on the strength of the relationship between the patient and the physician as per telehealth insurance website (The Doctor Insurance Agency, retrieved 11/05/2013). A proper explanation of how telehealth works and having a telehealth malpractice coverage is the best way to go.

Telehealth medical malpractice insurance companies have publicized examples of physicians working for self, groups, or a network of providers. These types of systems provide flexible work time for physicians with various experiences and various specialties and expertise. These groups of specialists are screened and credentialed before they are added to the specialist list. This kind of screening is performed up front so that the consumers are assured of the professional and quality services being provided to them and their family. On the other hand, patients gain by obtaining quicker appointment time at an affordable price to them and their employer while getting great care from the expert. This becomes a win-win situation when properly coordinated and managed.

Telemedicine and Telehealth Medical Malpractice Insurance Security and Compliance Security go hand in hand when it comes to the issue of Telemedicine / telehealth health insurance. Most insurance companies want to make sure that their insured clients are aware of their responsibilities in terms of compliance with HIPAA and all other patient privacy issues.

When speaking of medical malpractice insurance, some areas of concern in patient safety in telehealth are noted below:

- ✓ Medical licensure physicians and other health professionals are reminded to be compliant with state licensure of where their patients are located.
- ✓ Health-care providers should be familiar with the technology being used and/or have a department able to manage the technology.
- ✓ Health-care providers from a distance should have solid policy and procedure on how to manage communication and care continuum in case of equipment failure.
- ✓ Health-care providers should have proper and timely documentation in order to facilitate care coordination and care continuum.

Telehealth Medical Malpractice Insurance Coverage Highlights

- Telehealth medical malpractice insurance coverage available for physicians treating patients residing in all fifty states.
- Multiple state coverage available on same telehealth medical malpractice insurance policy.
- Policy premium based on time worked in each state.
- All specialties available including dermatology, pathology, internal medicine, radiology.
- Shared limit policy available for telehealth groups.
- Various telehealth medical malpractice insurance limit options to cover individual state requirements.
- Cyber insurance can be included to cover your increased privacy exposures due to operating over the Internet.
- Other policies also available to protect your normal practice telehealth exposures.

"We are rapidly becoming expert in the many areas of Telemedicine Medical Malpractice Insurance presented to owners and physician employees of telehealth practices: we will offer advice and competitive rates from a trusted liability carrier, working with doctors and their telehealth insurance needs" (The Doctor Insurance Agency, retrieved 11/05/2013).

The advice is to limit this type of communication to simple messages, like appointment confirmations, and leave the medical piece of information to secured sites where HIPAA law will be observed and patient information is protected.

Practitioners are afraid that they will be held liable for errors in data reported due to equipment malfunction or omission. Meanwhile, telehealth continues to be utilized in all kinds of care settings. These settings could be hospitals, home care, and doctor's offices, to all kinds of clinics, pharmacies, and nursing homes. Telehealth is used nationwide and worldwide. Telehealth is used in diagnosing diseases, providing care, teaching, consulting, conferencing, performing surgeries, and treating consumers of all kinds (Telemedicine Information Exchange: Electric News Net December 9, 2003). The ongoing debate is "How do you sue or discipline a professional who is not in the same state or country where an incident occurred?" Each state is given the leeway to uphold the law according to the state law and the nurse compact agreement between states.

CONFIDENTIALITY ISSUES

The issue of confidentiality is a hot topic in health care. The HIPAA regulations lay emphasis on the confidentialities in terms of information that is protected from third parties who are not connected to the care of the individual in question. Cloud security, as noted below, is recognized as an industry standard in guaranteeing secured access when rules and regulations concerning the use are followed.

Privacy and Security

HIPAA-compliant security measures ensure reliability and legally sound patient interaction. Encrypted access to session recordings and patient information from any Internet-connected computer is allowed with proper clearance via log-in identifications and password. With fully encrypted databases and all servers protected behind hardware firewall, this helps you make sure your patients' data are secured.

Privacy and Security measures are one of the reasons Cloud security is favored. Deploying cloud security is like keeping patients data under high security lock and key.

Patient Data Under Lock and Key

HIPAA compliance and patient privacy are our top priorities. The latest in data encryption is constantly deployed, distributed servers, and enterprise-class webhosting. Cloud Visit is an information fortress.

The other concern is the security of health-related information and the identifying information that is communicated via the Internet in the process of sending information to the intended destination. Telehealth is currently used in various areas, like wound monitoring; disease managements like CHF, diabetics, weight and HTN monitoring, wellness programs, and asthma programs; laboratory tests monitoring, like INR/ PT/PTT, and EKG; speech therapy; HHA supervision;

PT; psychiatric consultation; psychological consultation; teleradiology, etc. If you can think of it, you can do it through telehealth. The challenge of keeping all the records confidential while providing excellent care continues to be a challenge for distant sites. This could be local or international.

Telehealth has been proven to improve access to providers and resources located in a different geographic site. Expanding the use of telehealth allows health-care providers licensed in one state to provide consultations for patients located in a different state. A survey of 180 telehealth projects by the Council on Licensure, Enforcement, and Regulation (CLEAR) found that nearly every medical and nursing specialty is being practiced via long distance. Other specialties as well are engaged in such practices. The bottom-line advice is to follow HIPAA regulations. Most telehealth vendors are also following the banking industry's security system guideline in the transmission of health-care information. Transmission of health-care information is done through secured lines. Access is only given via user name and password.

The Verizon Terremark is one of the latest security measures of our modern technologies. "GET THE RIGHT LEVELS OF SECURITY TO THE RIGHT DEVICES, PEOPLE AND SYSTEMS WITH *VERIZON TERREMARK.* Learn how the scalability and power of the cloud can support your business mobility goals" (Verizon 2013).

Off-the-shelf videoconferencing products are being used as an entry point into the telehealth health-care market. These cost-effective products are cheap, and effective.

- Designation of Staff security level Access.
- Classify data based on risk and sensitivity levels.
- Protect data and assets with monitoring controls.

FINANCIAL ISSUES

There are several issues related to telehealth around which state legislation is focused. The first issue of concern is the cost of such programs. While telehealth is touted to increase access and decrease the cost of care, a recently released study for the Office of Rural Health Policy found that the combination of high start-up costs, steep transmission fees, and low volume made the typical electronic consultation an expensive session. However, anecdotal evidence indicates that once telehealth programs are in operation for several years, they can attract enough participation to bring down costs and improve access to care. Currently, hospitals, private insurances, and private pay are typical sources of funding. In addition, federal and state grants are also common sources of funding for telehealth programs.

The financial issue with telehealth is mostly the issue of funding the equipment. The initial up-front cost of establishing telehealth is often high. The various equipment necessary for initial setup are often expensive depending on the type that is chosen. Some of the delivery systems in use are as follows:

- *Plain old telephone system (POTS)*. This system involves transmission of information via the telephone line. This system is the most simple and least expensive that is currently available. Most of the equipment needed for this system is already in place for the employer: the phone line and the computer. The downside to this system is the slowness of the system and the restrictedness and nonflexibility of the system. Often, this system can only be used by one employee at a time.
- Videoconferencing system. This system involves transmission of information via video system. This system is often favored by the users and the patient. This system gives the user and the patient the ability to view and communicate with each other one-on-one. The ability to see what is going on on either side or what the patient is doing makes this a very good tool when accuracy in performance and return demonstration is crucial to the success of the teaching and healing of the patient. Being able to view the provider also gives the patient that psychological feeling of human touch, which is often one of the concerns of the patients and health-care providers when considering the implementation of the telehealth.

- Store-and-deliver system. This system involves storing the information at a designated server, and the information is transmitted to the health-care provider at a designated time. This system involves a process where the health-care provider or the patient uses the telehealth system and transmits the information to a designated server where the information is batched and stored for delivery at a designated time depending on how the system is programmed. The system could be programmed to store and deliver the information anywhere from every hour to once a day. This depends on the individual company and how critical the information delivery is to the care management of the patient population that the company is dealing with.

- Real-time system. This system transmits the collected data to the health-care provider immediately in real time. The real-time delivery system is often used in situations where the information is critical to the well-being of the patients. One such situation would be a situation whereby a patient is being monitored for high blood sugar and on sliding scale insulin, which is being adjusted by the primary physician. The blood sugar result would need to be transmitted to the health-care provider ASAP in real time in order for the appropriate dose of required insulin to be ordered and administered. For this type of result to be stored and delivered at a later time or at a later date would make it inappropriate since this type of result changes on a regular basis.

- Internet access. This system is a medium through which the information is retrieved or transmitted via the Internet. This system is fast and is able to transport a huge amount of information in a very short time. This process is performed locally, as in state to state, city to city, and internationally, as in country to country. This system also makes it possible for multiple users to access the information at the same time without delay. The Internet access is the most favored of all the mentioned systems because of all the advantages outlined above. Another advantage to the Internet access is the financial piece. Often, the Internet access is the most cost-effective of the systems that have been discussed so far. The Internet access is often secured at one flat rate. The company pays one flat rate for multiple unlimited accesses by its employee no matter their location. This is often considered a great deal by all means. Once the issue of security of the information on the Internet is taken care of, most companies would opt to go with the Internet access. Any health-care provider with the right user name and password will be able to retrieve the information that is entered into the Internet.

The other part of the financial story is the fact that most insurances do not pay for telehealth. It was just recently that Medicare and Medicaid started paying for the telehealth care at some states, with imposition of certain rules and regulations. Some states have made headway by approving telehealth payment by Medicaid.

Use below website for the telehealth Medicaid-approved states with their rules and regulations regarding use and payment for care:

http://www.americantelemed.org/policy/state-telemedicine-policy

Practitioners' and Patients' Attitude

Some practitioners and patients are late embracers of technological advancements. They do not believe it until it has been used, tested, and proven by other practitioners. This kind of attitude creates doubt in the mind of the consumers. These late adopters of the new technological ways of providing health care create a form of barrier for the quick advancement of the new technology. Once all these barriers are broken, the technology of telehealth will catch on like wildfire.

The Noncompatibility of the Different Equipment

Telehealth market is currently saturated by products from various companies working hard to dominate the market and hoping to land the next big contract. Some of the companies out there are HomMed, Ericon, AMAC, American TeleCare, AT&T, Verizon, etc. Each of these companies tries very hard to make their products unique and noncompatible with the product of their competitor. By so doing, these different companies are also creating a form of barrier to the advancement of telehealth technology. Once equipment is purchased, the purchasing company is sort of stuck with that equipment and that company. When the purchasing company decides to make a change due to growth or dissatisfaction with services, the purchasing company will not be able to switch easily because of the heavy cost of purchasing entirely new equipment. By making telehealth equipment compatible across company lines, the purchasing companies will be able to negotiate the best deals. They will also be more eager to invest in telehealth equipment. The compatibility will make it user-friendly because of the fact that the equipment that they bought from one company will be compatible with equipment from the new company as the need of the purchasing company changes. This kind of compatibility will boost the marketing of telehealth. The telehealth or telemedicine manufacturing markets are currently not user-friendly. Compatibility will make them more user-friendly. Each company is looking out for its own bottom line. They are in the market to make their product look good and produce the best product. The quest for making their products compatible with products from other companies is at the bottom of their list. By creating products that are compatible across companies, the manufacturers of the telehealth or telehealth equipment will boost the use of the telehealth products while helping with the advancement of health-care technology.

As more research is conducted on existing telehealth systems, both the private and public sectors are learning how to take full advantage of the benefits that telehealth has to offer to help improve the delivery of health-care services throughout the country. Over the past several years, states have begun to address legal issues related to the practice of telehealth. Georgia was one of the first states to pass legislation addressing telehealth. Georgia has sixty telemedical sites serving hospitals, correctional institutions, a public health facility, and an ambulatory health center. The National Governors' Association recently identified the Georgia Statewide Academic Medical System as the largest learning and telehealth network in the world. California appears to be a leader in this arena as well, having introduced legislation designating a state agency responsible for telehealth in 1994. California enacted the Telemedicine Development Act of 1996, which provides for licensure of out-of-state physicians, reimbursement for telehealth services, and oral and written patient consent for such services. Tennessee enacted legislation in 1996, creating special licenses to out-of-state physicians. Thus far, nineteen states are included as follows:

- Alabama
- Arkansas
- Colorado
- Connecticut
- Florida
- Georgia
- Hawaii
- Illinois
- Maryland
- Mississippi
- Montana
- Nebraska
- New Hampshire
- North Carolina
- North Dakota
- Ohio
- Oregon
- Rhode Island and Washington have introduced bills regarding the out-of-state licensure of physicians. The Colorado and Maryland bills

limit the amount of visits the out-of-state physician may have in one year without obtaining in-state licensure. A bill in Alabama as well as the bill in Maryland allows for the issuance of a "special purpose license," while a bill in North Dakota allows the issuance of a limited license. Bills in Ohio and Montana allow the issuance of a certificate to practice telehealth across state lines. The Ohio bill does not require a certificate if the nonresident physician is consulting twelve or fewer times a year. Bills in Arkansas, Connecticut, Florida, Georgia, Mississippi, Nebraska, New Hampshire, North Carolina, Oregon, and Rhode Island would require out-of-state physicians to be licensed within the state to practice medicine but would exempt physicians serving on a consultant basis. The Illinois bill allows out-of-state physicians from making a second opinion without obtaining a state medical license. The Washington bill allows an out-of-state physician to practice without a license in the state as long as the physician is sponsored by a physician licensed within the state. Only a few states reimburse for telehealth services. Ten of them are the following:

- Arkansas
- California
- Georgia
- North Dakota
- New Mexico
- Montana
- South Dakota
- Utah
- Virginia and West Virginia—provide Medicaid reimbursement.

In the following five states, Georgia, Kansas, Louisiana, Minnesota, and Pennsylvania, other insurance coverage is available. Arizona, Oklahoma, Texas, Louisiana, Mississippi, and Virginia introduced legislation this year to address reimbursement. The issue of telehealth is being driven by a multitude of constituencies, including legislators representing underserved populations who believe increased use of telehealth technology will increase access to health-care services. Telehealth is defined as a tool for improving access to health-care services and knowledge—not a clinical specialty practice.

On the federal level, ANA has taken a strong leadership role not only on behalf of all nurses but all health-care providers. ANA has initiated two national coalitions:

- Nursing organization's telehealth committee charged with developing guidelines for nurses to utilize when using telehealth as a tool to practice nursing.
- Interprofessional perspectives on telehealth standards.

ANA has endorsed a comprehensive telehealth initiative introduced into the US Senate by Senator Kent Conrad (D-ND). This proposal includes legislative language and definition of telehealth, which includes nurses as full practitioners and providers of telehealth. ANA has also identified many issues under the umbrella of telehealth, which require further study, including but not limited to the following:

- Nursing practice
- Ethical issues addressing confidentiality
- International issues and practicing in a world without boundaries
- Workplace issues related to collective bargaining
- Economic concerns
- Questions related to multistate licensure

NCSBN has also taken a lead in the latter issue as it pertains to telehealth. NCSBN reports that, increasingly, questions are being asked of state boards regarding the definition of nursing practice via a telecommunication device. State barriers to the practice of telehealth account for much of the attention the issue has recently received. The General Accounting Office states in their February 14, 1997, report, "The legal and regulatory barriers to implementing telehealth activities are licensure issues, malpractice liability, privacy and security, and regulation of medical devices." Approximately fifty-three bills related to telehealth have been introduced in twenty-nine states during the 1997 state legislative sessions. The scope of the legislation ranges from licensure of out-of-state physicians to data collection and reimbursement issues. As noted earlier in this report, many health-care professions are providing services through electronic networks; however, the majority of bills allow only physicians to provide and receive reimbursement for health-care services delivered via electronic means. Although nurses are specifically identified in some bills. Texas HB 2386 does provide for reimbursement for advanced practice nurses, and legislation in New Mexico would appropriate funds for a nurse distance-education program.

Secondly, the term *telehealth* is generally not defined in these bills. Arizona HB 2224, Oklahoma SB 48, and Texas HB 2033, however, do define telehealth as the practice of health-care delivery. As state legislators and regulators struggle with the concept of developing polices that best serve the public, nurses must continue to be involved in the debate. The practice of telehealth is not limited to physicians. Nursing is an integral component of the health-care delivery system and must be included in this emerging model of health-care delivery. (Further information on ANA's activities related to telehealth can be found in the House of Delegates report, status report on telenursing and telehealth.)

JCAHO Position on Telehealth

JCAHO has given each state the freedom to regulate their practice of telehealth. JCAHO Standard MS.4.120 basically states, "Licensed independent practitioners who are responsible for the care, treatment and services of the patients via telehealth link are subject to the credentialing and privileging process of the originating site." JCAHO Standard MS.4.130 also states, "The medical staffs at both the originating and distant sites recommend services to be provided by licensed independent practitioners through a Tele-medical link at their respective sites" (Makela 2004).

Below is the American Telemedicine Association legislation tracking as of February 2014. Go to www.ata.org website for up-to-date information.

The following is a list of medical license requirements to practice telehealth by state. The best advice is to always log on to the website for the latest information on licensing requirements.

Requirements may change without notice and are accurate to date of last review.

State	State Law/Regulation
Alabama (334) 242-4116 Website	Alabama has a Telemed license. (7) Special Purpose License. A special purpose license is a license issued by the Commission to practice medicine or osteopathy across state lines which: (a) Is only issued to an applicant whose principal practice location and license to practice is located in a state or territory of the United States whose laws permit or allow issuance of a special purpose license to practice medicine or osteopathy across state lines or a similar license to a physician whose principal practice location and license is located in the State of Alabama; (b) Limits the licensee solely to the practice of medicine or osteopathy across state lines as defined in these rules. (Chapter 540-X-16)
Alaska (907) 269-8163 **Website**	The Alaska Medical Board has issued an opinion that if the physician is licensed in another state and is reporting to another physician, he does not have to be licensed in Alaska. No specific telehealth law exists at this time.

**Arizona
(480)
551-2700
Website**

Physicians in Arizona who read and/or interpret medical records and radiology films must hold an Arizona license. Physicians residing in another state, federal jurisdiction or country who are authorized to practice medicine in that jurisdiction, are not required to hold an Arizona license if the physician engages in actual single or infrequent consultation with a doctor of medicine licensed in Arizona and if the consultation regards a specific patient or patients. A.R.S. 32-1421(B).

**Arkansas
(501)
296-1802
Website**

Physicians in Arkansas who read and/or interpret medical records and radiology films must hold an Arkansas license. Regulation No. 20 Practice of Medicine by a non-resident. Pursuant to Ark. Code. Ann 17-95-401 and 17-95-202, the Arkansas State Medical Board sets forth the following Rule and Regulation concerning the practice of medicine by a non-resident physicians or osteopaths: Any non-resident physician or osteopath who, while located outside the State of Arkansas, provides diagnostic or treatment services to patients within the State of Arkansas on a regular basis or under a contract with the health care provider, a clinic located in this state, or a health care facility, is engaged in the practice of medicine or osteopathy in this state and, therefore must obtain a license to practice medicine in this State. Any nonresident physician or osteopath who, while located outside of the state, consults on an irregular basis with a physician or osteopath who holds a license to practice medicine within the State of Arkansas and who is located in this State, is not required to obtain a license to practice medicine in the State of Arkansas. History: Adopted March 14, 1997

California
(916)
263-2389
Website

(1) A physician and surgeon practices medicine in this state across state lines when that person is located outside of this state but, through the use of any medium, including an electronic medium, practices or attempts to practice, or advertises or holds himself or herself out as practicing, any system or mode of treating the sick or afflicted in this state, or diagnoses, treats, operates for, or prescribes for any ailment, blemish, deformity, disease, disfigurement, disorder, injury, or other physical or mental condition of any person in this state. 2038. Whenever the words "diagnose" or "diagnosis" are used in this chapter, they include any undertaking by any method, device, or procedure whatsoever, and whether gratuitous or not, to ascertain or establish whether a person is suffering from any physical or mental disorder. Such terms shall also include the taking of a person's blood pressure and the use of mechanical devices or machines for the purpose of making a diagnosis and representing to such person any conclusion regarding his or her physical or mental condition. Machines or mechanical devices for measuring or ascertaining height or weight are excluded from this section.

12-36-106. Practice of medicine defined—exemptions from licensing requirements—repeal. (1) For the purpose of this article, "practice of medicine" means: (a) Holding out one's self to the public within this state as being able to diagnose, treat, prescribe for, palliate, or prevent any human disease, ailment, pain, injury, deformity, or physical or mental condition, whether by the use of drugs, surgery, manipulation, electricity, telehealth, the interpretation of tests, including primary diagnosis of pathology specimens, images, or photographs, or any physical, mechanical, or other means whatsoever; (g) The delivery of telehealth which means the delivery of medical services and any diagnosis, consultation, treatment, transfer of medical data, or education related to health care services using interactive audio, interactive video, or interactive data communication. Nothing in this paragraph (g) shall be construed to limit the delivery of health services by other licensed professionals, within the professional's scope of practice, using advanced technology, including, but not limited to, interactive audio, interactive video, or interactive data communication. (2) If any person who does not possess and has not filed a license to practice medicine within this state, as provided in this article, and who is not exempted from the licensing requirements under this section, shall do any of the acts mentioned in this section as constituting the practice of medicine, he shall be deemed to be practicing medicine without complying with the provisions of this article and in violation thereof.

**Colorado
(303)
894-7690
Website**

Connecticut
(860)
509-7603
Website

(d) The provisions of subsection (a) of this section shall apply to any individual whose practice of medicine includes any ongoing, regular or contractual arrangement whereby, regardless of residency in this or any other state, he provides, through electronic communications or interstate commerce, diagnostic or treatment services, including primary diagnosis of pathology specimens, slides or images, to any person located in this state. In the case of electronic transmissions of radiographic images, licensure shall be required for an out-of-state physician who provides, through an ongoing, regular or contractual arrangement, official written reports of diagnostic evaluations of such images to physicians or patients in this state. The provisions of subsection (a) of this section shall not apply to a nonresident physician who, while located outside this state, consults (A) on an irregular basis with a physician licensed by section 20-10 of the general statutes, as amended, who is located in this state or (B) with a medical school within this state for educational or medical training purposes. Notwithstanding the provisions of this subsection, the provisions of subsection (a) of this section shall not apply to any individual who regularly provides the types of services described in this subsection pursuant to any agreement or arrangement with a short-term acute care general hospital, licensed by the department of public health, provided such agreement or arrangement was entered into prior to February 1, 1996, and is in effect as of the effective date of this section. (e) On and after October 1, 1999, any person licensed as an osteopathic physician or osteopath pursuant to Chapter 371 shall be deemed licensed as a physician and surgeon pursuant to this chapter. (20-9)

Delaware
(302)
739-4522
Website

Telehealth is not mentioned in the current laws, but out of state physicians who do not fall into the category of a "consulting physician" have to have a license.

DC
(202)
724-4900
Website

There are no telehealth provisions at this time.

Florida (850)
245-4131
Website

64B8-9.010 Interpretation of Diagnostic Imaging Tests or Procedures. Physicians who order, perform, or interpret diagnostic imaging tests or procedures are responsible for the appropriateness and quality of the non-invasive diagnostic procedure, interpretation of the results, diagnosis, and either maintenance of medical records or provision of the results of the test to the referring physician. Specific Authority 458.309 FS. Law Implemented 458.331(1)(g), (m), (n), (t), (u), 766.111 FS. History New 11-4-93, Formerly 61F6-27.015, 59R-9.010.

Georgia
(404)
656-3913
Website

43-34-31.1. (a) A person who is physically located in another state or foreign country and who, through the use of any means, including electronic, radiographic, or other means of telecommunication, through which medical information or data is transmitted, performs an act that is part of a patient care service located in this state, including but not limited to the initiation of imaging procedures or the preparation of pathological material for examination, and that would affect the diagnosis or treatment of the patient is engaged in the practice of medicine in this state. Any person who performs such acts through such means shall be required to have a license to practice medicine in this state and shall be subject to regulation by the board. Any such out-of-state or foreign practitioner shall not have ultimate authority over the care or primary diagnosis of a patient who is located in this state. (b) This Code section shall not apply to: (1) The acts of a doctor of medicine or doctor of osteopathy located in another state or foreign country who: (A) Provides consultation services at the request of a physician licensed in this state; and (B) Provides such services on an occasional rather than on a regular or routine basis;

Hawaii
(808)
586-3000
Website

Hawaii does not specifically address telehealth but reading of films/x-ray images for a patient in Hawaii would be considered practicing medicine in the state and will therefore require a Hawaii medical license.

Idaho
(208)
327-7000
Website

The board often receives requests on whether physicians who regularly read radiologic or imaging studies done in Idaho on Idaho patients by Idaho physicians must have an Idaho license. It is the Board's interpretation that such physicians must hold an Idaho license. The "practice of medicine" means to investigate, diagnose, treat, correct, or prescribe for any human disease, ailment, injury, infirmity, deformity, or other condition, physical or mental, by any means or instrumentality. Idaho Code 54-1804(2) makes it a felony to practice in the state of Idaho without a license.

Sec. 49.5. Telehealth. (a) The General Assembly finds and declares that because of technological advances and changing practice patterns the practice of medicine is occurring with increasing frequency across state lines and that certain technological advances in the practice of medicine are in the public interest. The General Assembly further finds and declares that the practice of medicine is a privilege and that the licensure by this State of practitioners outside this State engaging in medical practice within this State and the ability to discipline those practitioners is necessary for the protection of the public health, welfare, and safety. (b) A person who engages in the practice of telehealth without a license issued under this Act shall be subject to penalties provided in Section 59. © For purposes of this Act, "telehealth" means the performance of any of the activities listed in Section 49, including but not limited to rendering written or oral opinions concerning diagnosis or treatment of a patient in Illinois by a person located outside the State of Illinois as a result of transmission of individual patient data by telephonic, electronic, or other means of communication from within this State. "Telehealth" does not include the following: (1) periodic consultations between a person licensed under this Act and a person outside the State of Illinois; (2) a second opinion provided to a person licensed under this Act; and (3) diagnosis or treatment services provided to a patient in Illinois following care or treatment originally provided to the patient in the state in which the provider is licensed to practice medicine. (d) Whenever the Department has reason to believe that a person has violated this Section, the Department may issue a rule to show cause why an order to cease and desist should not be entered against that person. The rule shall clearly set forth the grounds relied upon by the Department and shall provide a period of 7 days from the date of the rule to file an answer to the satisfaction of the Department. Failure to answer to the satisfaction of the Department shall cause an order to cease and desist to be issued immediately. (e) An out-of-state person providing a service listed in Section 49 to a patient residing in Illinois through the practice of telehealth submits himself or herself to the jurisdiction of the courts of this State (Source: P.A. 90-99, eff. 1-1-98).

Illinois
(312)
814-4500
Website

**Indiana
(317)
232-2960
Website**

IC 25-22.5-1-1.1 Definitions Sec. 1.1. As used in this article: (a) "Practice of medicine or osteopathic medicine" means any one (1) or a combination of the following: (1) Holding oneself out to the public as being engaged in: (A) the diagnosis, treatment, correction, or prevention of any disease, ailment, defect, injury, infirmity, deformity, pain, or other condition of human beings; (B) the suggestion, recommendation, or prescription or administration of any form of treatment, without limitation; (4) Providing diagnostic or treatment services to a person in Indiana when the diagnostic or treatment services: (A) are transmitted through electronic communications; and (B) are on a regular, routine, and non-episodic basis or under an oral or written agreement to regularly provide medical services.

**Iowa
(515)
281-5171
Website**

At a recent meeting, the Iowa Board of Medical Examiners reviewed the inquiry relating to the licensure requirements for out-of-state physicians performing diagnoses through electronic means. It is the Board's policy to require any physician who participates in the diagnosis and treatment of a patient situated in Iowa to obtain licensure. However, there is a provision in the Board's authorizing statute which permits physicians not licensed in Iowa to provide medical consultation and services which are "incidental" to the care of patients. Medical reports used for "primary diagnostic purposes" are generally not considered incidental and thus are seldom exempted under this provision.

**Kansas
(785)
296-7413
Website**

K.A.R. 100-26-1 addresses the issue, though it does not prohibit telehealth. Essentially, it requires Kansas licensure, or exemption from licensure, if the patient is located in Kansas, regardless of the doctor's location. Exemption from licensure is usually accomplished through consultation or supervision with a Kansas licensee. In short, the Board has generally believed that an initial read constitutes a diagnosis which requires licensure or supervision, and an over read is consultation which does not require licensure. New regulations are proposed, and have been adopted on a temporary basis, for other services performed within the state. Please find these regulations on our website at www.ksbha.org.

**Kentucky
(502)
429-7150
Website**

Telemedicine Policy Statement Physicians living outside Kentucky but actively practicing medicine upon patients within Kentucky should be required to meet the same statutory qualifications and should be held to the same standards of acceptable and prevailing medical practice within the Commonwealth as are resident physicians practicing within the state. Adopted: September 18, 1997

**Louisiana
(504)
568-6820
Website**

The Louisiana Medical Board has issued an opinion that the doctor has to be licensed in LA in order to practice telehealth.

**Maine
(207)
287-3601
Website**

No specific telehealth provision exists at this time, but the current law states: Unless licensed by the board, an individual may not practice medicine or surgery or a branch of medicine or surgery or claim to be legally licensed to practice medicine or surgery or a branch of medicine or surgery within the State by diagnosing, relieving in any degree or curing, or professing or attempting to diagnose, relieve or cure a human disease, ailment, defect or complaint, whether physical or mental, or of physical and mental origin, by attendance or by advice, or by prescribing or furnishing a drug, medicine, appliance, manipulation, method or a therapeutic agent whatsoever or in any other manner unless otherwise provided by statutes of this State [1995, c. 671, 11 (amd)].

Maryland
(410)
764-4777
Website

Maryland Medical Board is working on issuing a declatory ruling in the spring of 2006, then they plan on putting forth a telehealth law.

Massachusetts
(617)
654-9800
Website

There are no mentions of telehealth in the current law; however, the opinion of the Board is that the statute defines occasional consultation as once a year. Providing diagnosis on more frequent basis requires obtaining a state medical license.

Michigan
(517)
373-6873
Website

No specific mention of telehealth but the current law states that one is required to have a full license to practice medicine.

Minnesota
(612)
617-2130
Website

Minnesota offers a telehealth license, it is more restricted and costs less than a full medical license. Please call the board and request a telehealth application.

Mississippi
(601)
987-3079
Website

Full, unrestricted Mississippi license required for practice of telehealth. License is not required if reading for consultation only. 73-25-34. Telehealth licensing requirements for practicing medicine across state lines. (1) For the purposes of this section, telehealth or the practice of medicine across state lines, shall be defined to include any one or both of the following: (a) Rendering of a medical opinion concerning diagnosis or treatment of a patient within this state by a physician located outside this state as a result of transmission individual patient data by electronic or other means from within this state to such physician or his agent; or (b) The rendering of treatment to a patient within this state by a physician located outside this state as a result of transmission of individual patient data by electronic or other means from within this state to such physician or his agent. (2) Except as hereinafter provided, no person shall engage in the practice of medicine across state lines (telehealth) in this state, hold himself out as qualified to do the same, or use any title, word or abbreviation to indicate to or induce others to believe that he is duly licensed to practice medicine across state lines in this state unless he has first obtained a license to do so from the State Board of Medical Licensure and has met all educational and licensure requirements as determined by the State Board of Medical Licensure. (3) The requirement of licensure as set forth in subsection (2) above shall not be required where the evaluation, treatment and/or the medical opinion to be rendered by a physician outside this state (a) is requested by a physician duly licensed to practice medicine in this state, and (b) the physician who has requested such evaluation, treatment and/or medical opinion has already established a doctor/patient relationship with the patient to be evaluated and/or treated.

Missouri
(573)
751-0098
Website

Missouri Medical Board issued an opinion that one cannot practice any type of medicine in Missouri without a full medical license.

Montana
(406)
841-2300

Radiologists are exempt from licensure to diagnose for a medical condition by reading x-rays, etc. However, some facilities require physicians to obtain a license.

71-1,102. Practice of medicine and surgery, defined. For the purpose of the Uniform Licensing Law, and except as otherwise provided by law, the following classes of persons shall be deemed to be engaged in the practice of medicine and surgery: (1) Persons who publicly profess to be physicians, surgeons, or obstetricians, or publicly profess to assume the duties incident to the practice of medicine, surgery, or obstetrics, or any of their branches; (2) persons who prescribe and furnish medicine for some illness, disease, ailment, injury, pain, deformity, or any physical or mental condition, or treat the same by surgery; (3) persons holding themselves out to the public as being qualified in the diagnosis or treatment of diseases, ailments, pain, deformity, or any physical or mental condition, or injuries of human beings; (4) persons who suggest, recommend, or prescribe any form of treatment for the intended palliation, relief, or cure of any physical or mental ailment of any person; (5) persons who maintain an office for the examination or treatment of persons afflicted with ailments, diseases, injuries, pain, deformity, or any physical or mental condition of human beings; (6) persons who attach to their name the title of M.D., surgeon, physician, physician and surgeon, or any word or abbreviation indicating that they are engaged in the treatment or diagnosis of ailments, diseases, injuries, pain, deformity, infirmity, or any physical or mental condition of human beings; and (7) persons who are physically located in another state but who, through the use of any medium, including an electronic medium, perform for compensation any service which constitutes the healing arts that would affect the diagnosis or treatment of an individual located in this state, unless he or she is providing consultation services to a physician and surgeon who is duly licensed in this state and is a treating physician of the individual. For purposes of this subdivision, consultation means the evaluation of the medical data of the patient as provided by the treating physician and rendering a recommendation to such treating physician as to the method of treatment or analysis of the data (Source: Laws 1927, c. 167, 100, p. 482; C.S. 1929, 71-1401; Laws 1943, c. 150, 18, p. 546; R.S. 1943, 71-1,102; Laws 1969, c. 563, 1, p. 2291; Laws 1997, LB 452, 1. Effective date September 13, 1997).

Nebraska
(402)
471-2118
Website

Nevada
(775)
688-2559
Website

Nevada license is required. Physicians practicing telehealth may qualify for a special license, please call licensing at 775-688-2559 x233.

New
Hampshire
(603)
271-1203
Website

329:1-b Practice of Teleradiology. I. In this section, "teleradiology" means the evaluation, interpretation, or consultation by the electronic transmission of radiological images from one location to another. II. Any out-of-state physician providing radiological services who performs radiological diagnostic evaluations or interpretations for New Hampshire patients by means of Teleradiology shall be deemed to be in the practice of medicine and shall be required to be licensed under this chapter. III. This section shall not apply to out-of-state radiologists who provide consultation services pursuant to RSA 329:21, II (Source: 1999, 246:2, eff. Sept. 7, 1999).

New Jersey
(609)
826-7100
Website

New Jersey Medical Board has issued a policy that all physicians practicing medicine must hold a NJ license. A specific telehealth regulation is pending review.

New Mexico
(505)476-7220
Website

Yes, radiologists will need at least a telehealth license, $300 fee; will need to fill out a state-wide MD application, present verification of all licenses in other states (active, full and unrestricted), and physicians cannot be physically practicing in NM.

New York
(518)
474-3817 Ext.
560
Website

New York Medical Board has issued a statement on telehealth (click on link for more information). In the practice of medicine and dentistry, Education Law includes specific provisions permitting occasional consultations by physicians and dentists licensed in their home state (Education Law Section 6526(3) for medicine, and Section 6610(5) for dentistry). This consultation exemption statutorily establishes the extent to which these professionals licensed in other jurisdictions may practice in New York State when engaged in consulting arrangements. This regulatory approach is premised on the prohibition in law against professional practice in New York by anyone who is not licensed in this State.

North
Carolina
(919)
326-1100
Website

(b) Any person shall be regarded as practicing medicine or surgery within the meaning of this Article who shall diagnose or attempt to diagnose, treat or attempt to treat, operate or attempt to operate on, or prescribe for or administer to, or profess to treat any human ailment, physical or mental, or any physical injury to or deformity of another person. A person who resides in any state or foreign country and who, by use of any electronic or other mediums, performs any of the acts described in this subsection, including prescribing medication by use of the Internet or a toll-free telephone number, shall be regarded as practicing medicine or surgery and shall be subject to the provisions of this Article and appropriate regulation by the North Carolina Medical Board.

North Dakota
(701)
328-6500
Website

There is no specific regulation for telehealth, but a physician is said to be practicing medicine in the location of the patient, not the physician, and thus the state requires a full license.

Ohio
(614)
466-3934
Website

Statutes 4731.296 Telehealth certificate. (A) For the purposes of this section, "the practice of telehealth" means the practice of medicine in this state through the use of any communication, including oral, written, or electronic communication, by a physician located outside this state. (B) A person who wishes to practice telehealth in this state shall file an application with the state medical board, together with a fee in the amount of the fee described in division (D) of section 4731.29 of the Revised Code. The board may issue, without examination, a telehealth certificate to a person who meets all of the requirements. © The holder of a telehealth certificate may engage in the practice of telehealth in this state. A person holding a telehealth certificate shall not practice medicine in person in this state without obtaining a special activity certificate under section 4731.294 of the Revised Code.

Oklahoma
(405)
848-6841
Website

There is no specific regulation for telehealth, but the state requires a full license to practice any type of medicine.

Oregon
(503)
229-5770
Website

Radiologists do not need to obtain a license if they are practicing teleradiology only and are located outside of the state of Oregon. "A physician whose specialty is radiology or diagnostic radiology who practices in a location outside of Oregon and receives radiological images via teleradiology from an Oregon location for interpretation or consultation and who communicates his/her radiological findings back to the ordering physician may register and pay a biennial active registration fee. Licensee must file an affidavit before beginning active practice in Oregon."

Pennsylvania (717) 787-2381 Website

The Board does not currently have specific regulations addressing the parameters of how to engage in the practice of medicine over the Internet. Absent specific regulations physicians are obligated under Section 41 of the Medical Practice Act, 63 P.S. 422.41 to adhere to accepted standards of practice.

Puerto Rico (787) 782-8949

20 L.P.R.A. 6002 License; After the approval of this law any physician or osteopath that desires to practice telehealth in Puerto Rico has to apply for and obtain a license from the Board of Medical Examiners for the practice of medicine, surgery or osteopathy in compliance with the requirements of sections 31 and following of Chapter 20.

Rhode Island (401) 222-3855 Website

1.14 "Practice of Medicine," pursuant to section 5-37-1 (1) of the Act, shall include the practice of allopathic and osteopathic medicine. Any person shall be regarded as practicing medicine within the meaning of the act who holds himself or herself out as being able to diagnose, treat, operate, or prescribe for any person ill or alleged to be ill with disease, pain, injury, deformity or abnormal physical or mental condition, or who shall either profess to heal, offer or undertake, by any means or method, to diagnose, treat, operate, or prescribe for any person for disease, pain, injury, deformity or physical or mental condition. In addition, one who attaches the title M.D., physician, surgeon, D.O., osteopathic physician and surgeon, or any other similar word or words or abbreviation to his or her name indicating that he or she is engaged in the treatment or diagnosis of the diseases, injuries or conditions of persons shall be held to be engaged in the practice of medicine.

South Carolina (803) 896-4500 Website

It is the board's position that an out-of-state physician who renders a primary diagnosis on a patient physically located in this state is practicing medicine, as defined by state law, and must be licensed in South Carolina.

South Dakota
(605)
367-7781
Website

SL 1995, Ch 212, SL 2002, Ch. 175, 36-4-41. Practice of medicine or osteopathy in South Dakota while located outside of state. Any nonresident physician or osteopath who, while located outside this state, provides diagnostic or treatment services through electronic means to a patient located in this state under a contract with a health care provider licensed under Title 36, a clinic located in this state that provides health services, a health maintenance organization, a preferred provider organization, or a health care facility licensed under chapter 34-12, is engaged in the practice of medicine or osteopathy in this state. Consultation between a nonresident physician or osteopath and a licensee under this chapter is governed by 36-2-9.

Tennessee
(615)
532-3202
Website

0880-2-.05 LICENSURE OF OUT-OF-STATE AND INTERNATIONAL APPLICANTS. To practice medicine in Tennessee a person must possess a lawfully issued license from the Board. The Board in its discretion may issue licensure based upon licensure in another state or distinguished faculty status according to the following criteria, process and qualifications: (6) If an applicant has ever held a license to practice medicine in any other state or Canada, the applicant shall submit or cause to be submitted the equivalent of a Tennessee Certificate of Endorsement from each such licensing board which indicates the applicant either holds a current active medical license and whether it is in good standing, or has held a medical license which is currently inactive and whether it was in good standing at the time it became inactive; 0880-2-.16 TELEMEDICINE LICENSURE. No person shall engage in the practice of medicine across state lines in this State, hold himself out as qualified to do the same, or use any title, word, or abbreviation to indicate to or induce others to believe that he is licensed to practice medicine across state lines in this State unless he is actually so licensed in accordance with the provisions of this rule.

Texas **(512)** **305-7010** **Website**	Telehealth provisions: © State Licensure. Physicians who treat and prescribe through the Internet are practicing medicine and must possess appropriate licensure in all jurisdictions where patients reside. (Click on the link for more information)
Utah **(801)** **530-6628** **Website**	(2) Regardless of the form in which a licensee engages in the practice of medicine, the licensee may only permit the practice of medicine in that form of practice to be conducted by an individual: (a) licensed in Utah as a physician and surgeon under Section 58-67-301 or as an osteopathic physician and surgeon under Section 58-68-301; and (b) who is able to lawfully and competently engage in the practice of medicine.
Vermont **(802)** **657-4220** **Website**	There are no specific telehealth provisions, but the current law states that to practice any type of medicine one needs a full medical license of the state.
Virginia **(804)** **662-9908** **Website**	There are no telehealth provisions at this time.
Washington **(360)** **236-4788** **Website**	When an out of state radiologist is the only radiologist reading the film, i.e., no second in house read, then the radiologist is practicing medicine in Washington. In reviewing this issue with the AAG advisers we have always agreed that RCW 18.71.030 (6) is the justification for not requiring that the out of state radiologist (or pathologist) have a Washington license. Sub (6) requires that the MD be licensed in another state or territory (this means a US territory such as the Virgin Islands) so that excludes radiologists or pathologists residing and practicing in England, Australia, India etc. The board would advise that hospitals contracting with out of state providers require that in addition to holding a valid US license, the utilized providers be board certified by the American Board of Medical Specialties (ABMS).

30-3-13. Unauthorized practice of medicine and surgery or podiatry; criminal penalties; limitations. (a) A person shall not engage in the practice of medicine and surgery or podiatry, hold himself or herself out as qualified to practice medicine and surgery or podiatry or use any title, word or abbreviation to indicate to or induce others to believe that he or she is licensed to practice medicine and surgery or podiatry in this state unless he or she is actually licensed under the provisions of this article. A person engaged in the practice of telemedicine is considered to be engaged in the practice of medicine within this state and is subject to the licensure requirements of this article. As used in this section, the term "practice of telehealth" means the use of electronic information and communication technologies to provide health care when distance separates participants and includes one or both of the following: (1) The diagnosis of a patient within this state by a physician located outside this state as a result of the transmission of individual patient data, specimens or other material by electronic or other means from within this state to the physician or his or her agent; or (2) the rendering of treatment to a patient within this state by a physician located outside this state as a result of transmission of individual patient data, specimens or other material by electronic or other means from within this state to the physician or his or her agent. No person may practice as a physician's assistant, hold himself or herself out as qualified to practice as a physician's assistant, or use any title, word or abbreviation to indicate to or induce others to believe that he or she is licensed to practice as a physician's assistant in this state unless he or she is actually licensed under the provisions of this article. Any person who violates the provisions of this subsection is guilty of a misdemeanor and, upon conviction thereof, shall be fined not more than ten thousand dollars, or imprisoned in the county jail not more than twelve months, or both fined and imprisoned. (b) The provisions of this section do not apply to: (2) Physicians or podiatrists licensed in other states or foreign countries who are acting in a consulting capacity with physicians or podiatrists duly licensed in this state, for a period of not more than three months: Provided, That this exemption is applicable on a one-time only basis;

**West Virginia
(304)
558-2921
Website**

**Wisconsin
(608)
266-2112
Website**

448.01(9) (9) "Practice of medicine and surgery" means: 448.01(9)(a) (a) To examine into the fact, condition or cause of human health or disease, or to treat, operate, prescribe or advise for the same, by any means or instrumentality.

**Wyoming
(307)
778-7053
Website**

(e) No exemption from licensure for out-of-state physicians. Any physician rendering medical diagnosis and/or treatment to a person physically present in this state must have a license issued by the board when such diagnosis/treatment is rendered, regardless of the physician's location and regardless of the means by which such diagnosis/treatment is rendered. This regulation shall not apply if an out-of-state physician consults by telephone, electronic or any other means with an attending physician licensed by this board or an out-of-state physician is specifically exempt from licensure under W.S. 33-26-103(a)(i-ix). Section 7. Exemption from licensure. (a) Consultants. Physicians residing in and licensed to practice medicine in another state or country called into this state for consultation by a physician licensed to practice medicine in this state may practice medicine without first obtaining a Wyoming license for a period not to exceed seven (7) days in any fifty-two (52) week period. Consults of longer duration or greater frequency are not exempt and require licensure. (www. healthcareitnews.com/blog/**state-state-telemedicine-licensure**, retrieved 9/25/2013)

1 *Last updated: August 2012, please log on to the various websites for updates.*

Telehealth Overview

Board-by-Board Approach

Document Summary:

- Ten (10) state boards issue a special purpose license, telehealth license or certificate, or license to practice medicine across state lines to allow for the practice of telehealth.

- Fifty-seven (57) state boards plus the DC Board of Medicine require that physicians engaging in telehealth are licensed in the state in which the patient is located.
- Minnesota allows physicians to practice telehealth if they are registered to practice telehealth or are registered to practice across state lines.
- Nineteen (19) states require private insurance companies to cover telehealth services to the same extent as face-to-face consultations.
- Massachusetts permits coverage for services provided through telehealth as long as the deductible, copayment or coinsurance doesn't exceed the deductible, copayment or coinsurance applicable to an in-person consultation.

State	Type of License Required	Legislation/Regulations/Policy Guidelines	Pending Legislation/Notes

AL	Board can issue a special purpose license to practice across state lines upon application.	No person shall engage in the practice of medicine or osteopathy across state lines in this state, hold himself or herself out as qualified to do the same, or use any title, word or abbreviation to indicate to or induce others to believe that he or she is licensed to practice medicine or osteopathy across state lines in this state unless he or she has been issued a special purpose license to practice medicine or osteopathy. ALA. CODE § 34-24-502.
		The commission shall only issue a special purpose license to practice medicine or osteopathy across state lines to an applicant whose principal practice location and license to practice is located in a state or territory of the United States whose laws permit or allow for the issuance of a special purpose license to practice medicine or osteopathy across state lines or similar license to a physician whose principal practice location and license is located in this state. It is the stated intent of this article that physicians and osteopaths who hold a full and current license in the State of Alabama be afforded the opportunity to obtain, on a reciprocal basis, a license to practice medicine or osteopathy across state lines in any state or territory of the United States as a pre-condition to the issuance of a special purpose license as authorized by this article to a physician or osteopath licensed in such state or territory. The State Board of Medical Examiners shall determine which states or territories have reciprocal licensure requirements meeting the qualifications. ALA. CODE § 34-24-507.
AK	Must obtain an Alaska license.	"Telehealth" means the practice of health care delivery, evaluation, diagnosis, consultation, or treatment, using the transfer of medical data, audio, visual or data communications.

(**"telemedicine_licensure"** cached www.fsmb.org/pdf/grpol)_

REVIEW OF RELATED LITERATURE

"But why think about that when all the golden land's ahead of you and all kinds of unforeseen events wait lurking to surprise you and make you glad you're alive to see? (Kerouac 2004)"

"Communication is about connecting surgeons and other medical professionals with the information they need. We make systems that link operating rooms with facilities around the world—and we support them with a range of integrated surgical equipments, lights and booms. These systems exchange MRIS, X. rays, live pictures and other kinds of information between operating rooms, doctors, offices and teaching institutions everywhere. The goal is making telehealth a reality in real time, with worldwide access" (communication site map, Stryker-2004 61).

Tele is the Greek word for "far off" or, as Webster's dictionary defines it, "distance," or "remote." As far back as 1948, radiological images were communicated across distances. It was documented that x-rays were transmitted over telephone lines between West Chester and Philadelphia, Pennsylvania. By 1959, it was also documented that the University of Nebraska used two-way closed-circuit television to transmit visual images of neurological examinations for medical education. By 1962, the University of Nebraska had established a two-way microwave connection to the Nebraska Psychiatric Institute and the Norfolk State Hospital, which is one hundred (100) miles away. For the next six years, the system was used for consultation, and this was documented as the first successful interactive videoconferencing in the history of telehealth. The success of the early first generation of telehealth is part of the reason telehealth is regarded as a success in recent history. The documented success of the early embracers of telehealth gave the nation the green light to move forward and to continue to explore and embrace this field called telehealth. Telehealth clinical settings progress occurred in late 1960s. By 1968, clinical care projects were starting to get established in the United States. One of the notable clinical care projects was established between Massachusetts General Hospital and Boston's Logan International Airport's clinical station. The stations were staffed by nurse clinicians, and the patients were attended to via video-interactive system. This saved the cost of transporting the patients from the airport to the medical center. This also helped to expedite the assessment and treatment time. It was also documented that Massachusetts General Hospital expanded its services to include dermatology, radiology, cardiology, and telepsychiatry. These are the few early specialties that were established and utilized in the telehealth field. The field has grown today to include as many specialties as there are in the health-care industry (Viegas and Dunn 1998).

Literature review on telehealth revealed that teleheath are in all the continents as noted below. The use could vary based on the political, knowledge, and comfort level of the powers that be, but the one constant is the evidence of increased use and the fact that the world is on board with this technology of health-care delivery.

Asian Connection

"Review of the literature on Tele-health in Asia was searched, out of the 1504 abstracts retrieved, 109 articles were selected by two independent reviewers for the final review. The number of published articles on Tele-health in Asia increased during the review period. The largest number of studies was conducted in Japan (37%). Most Tele-health applications were based on the store-and-forward modality (43%), with 35% using videoconferencing and 15% using a hybrid approach. Most of the studies were descriptive (75%) and only eight included a control group against which Tele-health was compared. The most common means of telecommunication was ISDN lines, which were employed in 32% of the studies. Some 40% of the studies mentioned improved quality of health care; about 20% mentioned improved access to health care. Although most studies mentioned cost, only 13 of them assessed resource utilization and cost. The overall findings gave a generally optimistic picture of Tele-health in Asia. However, there is a lack of good quality studies" (Dr. Hammad Durrani, The Royal Society of Medicine Journals July 2013).

African Connection

Questions remain as to whether telehealth provides the most cost-effective solution in areas where resources are scarce and simply meeting the basic health needs of the population is of utmost priority, as is the case in the majority of developing countries. Although there is currently a conspicuous difference in the level of telehealth implementation between high-income and low-income countries, it is encouraging to note the desire in some developing countries to implement telehealth solutions at an informal level (i.e., using telehealth services in an ad hoc fashion), particularly within the African and Eastern Mediterranean regions. Such a desire illustrates recognition of the potential for telehealth to make a positive impact on health care in the developing world, provided the right conditions are present. That these initiatives are still at an informal level could reflect the fact that to be technically feasible they must be scaled to parallel the available infrastructure and ICT capacity. When resources such as electricity, access to communication systems, or personnel are scarce, telehealth initiatives should use these resources as efficiently as possible (*WHO 2010, retrieved 9/9/2013*).

Australian Connection

"Telehealth around the world, and in Australia, is currently focused on specialist consultation to patients in rural and remote locations. It concentrates on selected medical specialties, which are least compromised by the limitations associated with video-consultation. In most services, (relatively expensive) hardware video-conferencing equipment is utilized" (Uni-Quest Report 16807, Tele-health Assessment Final Report 28 June 2011, p. 5).

Our scan of global online health strategies does not reveal a common or core group of services that should be provided by *national* telehealth services. Service evolution appears to gain prominence from first mover advantage, from clearly defined rural and from political demands.

Videoconference

Videoconferencing has gained popularity with the advent of various smart phones and the reduction in pricing of videoconferencing equipment.

Funding of this form of telemedicine, or telehealth has also increased. What is clear is that in situ medico-political turbulence provides the impetus and government provides some or all the funding. The private sector, as a general rule, tends to be idiosyncratic and driven by value-added opportunities. By way of example, the Indian private health-care market delivery via video is more advanced than is the case in Australia with Apollo Health being the leading exponent.

The main systemic expansion areas associated with the Australian health system are the following:

- A well-funded desire to address mental health service divides especially between rural and urban areas with a focus on depression

- A restructure of the aged care system and strengthening the current policy setting associated with aging in place
- Deliberate but undirected funding for telehealth
- Underfunding for a personally controlled electronic health record (PCEHR)
- The emerging opportunities to deliver health and wellness services via the National Broadband Network

A national telehealth framework must deliberately focus on a set of manageable telehealth services that will deliver the greatest health and wellness outcome. Our scan of the available material and our understanding of the Australian health system lead us to make the following recommendation as regards to whole-of-system focus areas.

Recommendation 1: Focus Areas

Broad health system areas of high impact relate to the following:

- Encouraging home-based access to care for the aged, the disabled, and selected others
- Addressing acute sector waiting lists by providing online bookings and status alerts
- Improving access to specialists for rural General Practitioners (GP) and allied health providers
- Need to support national programs proving new care-delivery models for mental health and aged care
- Integration of primary and allied health
- Specialist access for key conditions such as oncology
- Pre—and postnatal maternity services

These concerns translate to health-care delivery processes in the following areas:

- Home-based rehabilitation, drug management, and postoperative wound care.
- Acute care services booking online and improved collaboration for team-based care delivery via joint coordination and electronic alerts.
- Access and reach to key services in rural areas associated with mental health (depression counseling in particular), dementia assessment, and care and clinical staff in-service training.
- Improved coordination and provision of mental health services and aged care support services in metropolitan and regional areas.

- The ability of GPs, specialists, and those clinicians in the public health sector to collaborate and consult in both real time and via store and forward methods.
- Provide patients in both rural and urban areas with better access to specialist services, educational material, and online peer-group support via portals—examples being virtual maternity and aged care.

The relative impact of each focus area is displayed below:

The widespread use of the Internet means that availability of innovative web tools and processes (web 2.02) to assess, monitor, evaluate, collaborate, and explore medical conditions by **both** patients and practitioners is a reality. There is a wealth of sites and tools currently available, but the level of innovation is yet to explode.

There is a quiet revolution going on. It is a revolution about information access, equity of access, and participatory medicine. The old adage that the doctor knows best is being questioned, initially by those of the baby-boomer generation but especially by the millennials. The huge increase in the incidence of complex chronic disease means that primary care practitioners simply are unable to keep up with the latest research and new modes of treatment and, in Australia, rarely participate in team-based care provision. Our primary model is one of lone practitioners providing services in sequence.

The ability of web 2.0 technologies and social networking sites to merge and mix health data, personal information, and other types of information (commonly known as mash-ups) combined with the increasing popularity of mobile devices suggests that medical doctors, nurses, allied health professionals, and patients, along with their careers, may well be pushed down innovative ways of building new health-care delivery models. What is increasingly evident is that the demand by patients and their caregivers for better access, for better tools, and to engage in the dialogue about their own care is strong and increasing.

These considerations suggest that telehealth is more than the delivery of health-care services. It is about tailoring social networking to support health and wellness activities of both providers and receivers. The increasing use of telemonitoring, such as a patient wearing a twenty-four-hour ECG pack, will increase and will stimulate greater patient participation. There are literally hundreds of software tools available for users of smart phones, addressing everything from fitness to pain management.

It is our view that telehealth as a series of delivered solutions will soon be taken over by platform-based services offering a variety of tools and customizable services including social networking.

The current debate around Cloud computing is reflective of this transition. One significant implication of this is that data collected at the platform level can potentially be repurposed and reused across a variety of health and fitness settings (Michael Gill et al., A National Tele-health Strategy for Australia, retrieved 9/09/2013).

European Connection

In the United Kingdom, the government's care services minister, Paul Burstow, has stated that telehealth and telecare would be extended over the next five years (2012-2017) to reach three million people (*Wikipedia*, retrieved 9/10/2013).

Worldwide Connection

Fueled by health-care reform aimed at reducing in-patient cost and post acute care strategies designed to reduce readmissions, the worldwide telehealth (remote patient monitoring) market was predicted to had grown by 55% in 2013 in terms of device and service revenues, according to a recent report from InMedica, the medical technology research division of UK-based market research consultancy IMS Research.

InMedica's 2013 forecast is significantly higher than the telehealth growth rates seen in recent years. From 2010 to 2011, the firm's research found that telehealth usage worldwide increased by 22.2 percent. However, telehealth device revenues only grew by 5 percent over that same time span; they grew 18 percent from 2011 to 2012. InMedica attributed the slow revenue growth over the last year to "poor economic conditions leading to restrictions in healthcare funding particularly in Europe, and ambiguity on the impact of healthcare reform and readmission penalties on Tele-health in the U.S."

As leverage to push health-care providers to implement effective postacute care plans such as telehealth, the Centers for Medicare & Medicaid Services in October 2012 began penalizing US hospitals for re-admissions. Shane Walker, coauthor of the InMedica report, believes that telehealth is a tool that can significantly improve clinical outcomes while also achieving the long-term goals of CMS to move toward greater continuity of care while reducing costs through the avoidance of unnecessary duplication.

Despite the fact that telehealth has been in use since 1948, the cost and technological difficulties associated with the operation of the equipment prevented the widespread use of telehealth. As we moved toward the 1980s and the 1990s, the improvement in technology and the lowering costs of the telehealth equipment made it an attractive and affordable addition to the modern-day health-care delivery practice. The ability to use single or multiple equipment depending on the need of the patient has also made telehealth an attractive and affordable addition to the health-care technological system.

Telehealth can run the gamut from a simple reading of EKG via a telephone line, consultation over the video system, use of fax machine to deliver medical documents, to performance of operation at a remote distance via video guidance. Telehealth is used for various purposes. These purposes may include monitoring hotlines in the emergency department, dispensing medication six hundred miles away with a push of a button, to a sophisticated videoconferencing from different parts of the world. All these and more are some of the possibilities in the current world of telemedicine or telehealth. The convenience of the web and the ability to reach a larger population of the world makes telehealth an efficient and lucrative way of administering and advertising health care.

Just like any event that takes place on the web, there are pros and cons that need to be considered. The danger that lies ahead when telehealth are conducted via the web or when shopping online for health care is the danger of the unknown. The true facts of the credentials of the "online providers" may be difficult to verify. This uncertainty has its own repercussions for the consumers as well as the practitioners. This uncertainty could also spell disaster for both parties. There are different health-care groups like the American Medical Association and the National Association Board of Pharmacists out there who are working hard to address this important aspect of delivering care via telehealth (Terry, NP Fall 1999).

There are other methods of monitoring via telehealth that do not involve the use of the website. These are done via local telephone lines. These methods are better controlled in terms of confidentiality and compliance with HIPAA regulations. The downside to this is as follows:

- It is very limited in its ability to provide multiple access, real-time results and information.
- It is not cost-effective in transmission of large material.
- The transmission process is very slow and time-consuming.
- Access through the web accomplishes all of the above.

The web access has a major issue with security despite all its advantages. The security issues on the web access are being addressed by various companies at various levels. Some of the ways that issues of security are being addressed by various companies are as follows:

- Installation of secured access such as those used by the banking industries.
- The secured sites only allow people with authorized user access code and authorized passwords and user names to gain access to the website. The security issues are further addressed by giving limited access at different

levels of the organization depending on the need to know. This is the same system utilized at the different levels of the government and the CIA. Simply stated, this is a system whereby if you do not have the need to know, your access to the information is denied or limited to only the required information that you need to function at your level in the organization. For example, if you are a clinician who is not involved in the direct care of a patient, you do not have a need to know about this patient's medical condition. For this reason, your organization has the right to restrict your access to such information. Organizations are also becoming smart in monitoring their employees in order to fish out who is looking at what. Most companies are able to track employee movement on their intranet system. This is a built-in system whereby all activities to intranet sites could be traced back to a specific employee via their password and user codes. This is why all employees are usually advised not to share their user names and passwords for security purposes. Most companies also request that their employee change their password on a monthly basis. These are all a form of control that companies are putting in place to help control and maintain security on the intranet and Internet sites.

Due to HIPAA law, security issues are not just a necessity, they are required by law. Companies do not want to be sued, nor do they want to be sanctioned by the government, so they are putting a lot of emphasis on security issue. Security of medical information and privacy issue for the patients are a requirement in the United States. The HIPAA law in the United States even required that all health-care facilities and organizations conduct formal training for all their staff. Organizations that refuse to comply are often sanctioned by the government.

The health-care budget is climbing every day while the population continues to age. As the cost of care rises, the solution to rising health-care cost is not simple nor is it cheap. This rising cost of health care has affected several states, and each state is looking to find ways to cut health-care costs. Some states have found creative ways to cut health-care costs, like institution of telehealth, while other states simply cut programs that cater to the elderly and the poor. The irony to these types of cuts is the fact that the people who need the services the most are the very people whose services are sacrificed due to budget crunch and health-care crisis (Holahan John et al., "State Responses to Budget Crisis in 2004: An Overview of Ten States" January 2004).

Some of the other barriers that has been attributed to the slowdown of telehealth are *licensing*. Telehealth is practiced across state and country borders. Licensing for health-care professionals is different from state to state and also different from country to country. This has raised a lot of questions in general. There is an ongoing debate on how a practitioner should be licensed in order for him or her to be able to practice telehealth across states and across international borders.

There have been no easy answers to these questions, but they are being addressed by different health-care organizations. The professionals in the United States are licensed by each state, while their Canadian counterparts are licensed by each province. Either way you look at it, both countries have the need to find a level ground for its health-care professionals who want to practice telehealth. These practitioners need to be deemed competent to practice across borders without the undue burden of multiple licensures. This type of scenario holds true for other nations that are participants in this field of practicing health care called telehealth ("Tele-health: Great Potential or Risky Terrain?" *Nursing Now: Issues and Trends in Canadian Nursing,* Nov 2000, n. 9).

The National Association of Boards of Pharmacy (NABP) started addressing this issue with the recommendation that a registered pharmacist who is interested in practicing telepharmacy pay a registration fee to join a multistate registry of telepharmacists. This in turn will provide a data bank for verification of licensure in good standing for the telepharmacists. This system of registration will cut down on the burdensome process of getting licensure in each state where the telepharmacist plans to practice.

Streamlining the licensing process will also act as an incentive for telehealth practitioners to get involved in telehealth practice. The medical society and the nursing society have not reached a consensus on the final word about licensure. Most of the states have addressed the licensing issue on a local level. Majority of these states have set their own local rules while other states have no rules at all.

Malpractice Issues

Practitioners are afraid that they will be held liable for errors in data reported due to equipment malfunction or omission. Malpractice issue is nothing new in health care in general. Telehealth has taken this issue to the next level. This is due to the fact that it is different from the traditional system of health-care delivery. This issue gets complicated as we enter the world of telehealth. This is because practicing health-care delivery in cyberspace may create complications due to different laws in different states. This issue will be elaborated on in further discussions, and this reference will be utilized extensively.

Golden Advice in Managing Telehealth, Telemedicine or Electronic Health by Experienced Telehealth Nurses

There are suggestions given by experienced nurses in the field of telehealth system to assist the health-care provider in minimizing errors in the process of delivery care via telehealth or electronic health system. Some of the advices are as follows:

- Put the patient's welfare first.
- Use leading questions while interacting with the patient.
- Avoid use of medical terminology or jargon that will confuse the patient.
- Avoid jumping to conclusions.
- Avoid spending too little time with the patients.
- Avoid accepting the patient's self-diagnosis.
- Avoid not getting enough information from the patient.
- Avoid persisting with a telephone assessment when there is a language barrier ("Tele-health: Great potential or risky terrain?" *Nursing Now: Issues and Trends in Canadian Nursing* Nov 2000, n. 9).
- Use a certified medical translator via phone or in person as much as possible.
- Provide privacy during telehealth sessions.
- Document your encounter immediately or within twenty-four hours.

- Follow your institutional policies.
- Keep abreast of the current telehealth laws and policies, and amend your institutional policies accordingly.
- Seek to assist the patient to schedule a follow-up as soon as possible with the appropriate professional when there is a need for it based on your telehealth encounter.

The above pointers will be elaborated on as telehealth is explored further. The majority of telehealth equipment is portable, user-friendly, and is able to assist with monitoring physiological indices and deliver the data directly to a computer server. Others are able to monitor and deliver a just-in-time result. This is usually the case when videoconferencing equipment is utilized. Some of the physiological indices that are monitored by these equipment are as follows:

- Blood pressure
- Pulse rates
- Weight
- Blood oxygen and saturation level
- Glucose level
- PT/PTT
- Electrocardiogram

These machines are said to be cost-effective in helping the different programs that used them effectively. These programs are utilized at various health-care settings, such as hospitals, home care, managed care agencies, community health-care centers, private offices, etc.

I have also added some advice for the health-care recipients as follows:

You, as the patient or the health-care recipient, need to know your right as a health-care consumer. It is okay for you not to know about certain medical issues or terminologies, but it is not okay for you not to ask questions; continue asking as many times as possible until you get the answers to your questions. Remember that the health-care provider is providing care to many patients or many health-care receivers, but you are seeking answers to your particular symptom or illness. You deserve to receive care and get your questions answered.

Health-Care Receiver Suggested Guide to Receiving Telehealth, Telemedicine or Electronic Health Care

- Have a primary physician if possible.
- Create a health journal with all your basic health information.

- List all your medications.
- List your allergies.
- List your medical conditions.
- List the physicians' names and phone numbers who are involved in your care.
- Establish an online relationship with your doctor or doctor's office or your health-care professional team.
- Ask questions regarding the processes followed by your health-care provider.
- Are your health-care providers telehealth savvy? Ask questions.
- Are they practicing store and forward?
- Do they participate in videoconferencing?

The answers to these questions will help you, the health-care receiver, to get the most out of the teleheath system experience.

Some telehealth manufacturing companies are currently not as user-friendly as they should be. Each manufacturing company of telehealth is practically looking out for their own bottom line. They are in the market to make their product look good and produce the best product. The quest for making their products compatible with products from other companies is at the bottom of their list. Some of the equipment that are used in telemonitoring are excellent. The excellent equipment are user-friendly, and they are the equipment that are taking over the telehealth market. Some of the big names out there whose equipment are taking over the markets are as follows:

- AMAC
- AMC
- American TeleCare
- AT&T Digital Life
- In Touch Health
- LifeSize
- Philips
- Vericon

The benefits of telehealth or electronic health can be measured in health benefits and also in dollars and cents. As noted below, telehealth or electronic health can be utilized in monitoring various health situations as noted below:

This is a program where an intensive care unit is electronically monitored from a distance by physicians specialized in monitoring intensive care unit patients. Instead of being on-site at one hospital, these physicians are able to monitor multiple patients at multiple locations from a remote site. This system of patient management can reduce severity-adjusted length of stay, allowing hospitals to reduce costs and increase revenue. The debate about health-care costs has its solution tied to telehealth or electronic health.

Electronic ICU can be staffed from a remote site by specialists. The fact that the specialist is from a remote site makes it possible for the specialist to be available to multiple sites at a given time. The specialist can be tapped into locally or internationally as needed.

As noted below, there is evidence of cost savings associated with e-ICU. These cost savings more than paid for itself. There is also the added benefit of patient satisfaction. The reduction in discharge to postacute settings is an added savings, in addition to having a patient go to their homes as opposed to making another journey to a postacute facility. The eICU users have experienced the following:

- A $5,000 average cost savings per ICU patient[1]
- More patients discharged to home rather than to a postacute facility[2]

---

[1]   Zawada, et al., "Impact of an Intensive Care Unit Telemedicine Program on a Rural Health Care System," *Postgraduate Medicine* 3, 121(2009):162.

[2]   TeleICU project with University of Massachusetts Memorial Medical Center, NEHI Research Update, November 17, 2008.

Benefits of Telehealth, Telemedicine or Electronic Health

Studies have shown that proper utilization of telehealth health system has produced the following results:

- reduced health-care professional shortage
- improved care
- cut cost
- boosted health-care recipient's satisfaction
- increased user's knowledge of their disease process
- provided users with the educational knowledge necessary to understand and manage their diseases better

There is also push for evidence-based practice. Telehealth has come a long way to be identified as evidence-based practice. There are many examples of effective deployment of telehealth by various companies. For example, AMC has published their evidence-based results as noted on their website below:

The following are some of their reported evidence-based results:

- Reduction in hospitalization by two digits.
- Reduction in costs of managing chronic illnesses.
- Effective in managing CMS triple-aim standard of care, i.e., better care, better health, low cost.
- User-friendly equipment are also making this system of health care very timely and cost-effective.

There is also evidence that a well-informed staff and consumer will manage the telehealth system better, and this in turn will increase utilization and save money.

Benefits of Cloud Visit?

There are many reasons to choose Cloud Visit as your telehealth / telepsychiatry provider. With our simple and intuitive web interface, transparent pricing model, and easy setup, the question is: Why not?

Easy, safe, and affordable telemedicine

At the same time, your patients receive the same quality, face-to-face care as in office visits, without the hassle and expense of travel.

You'll be up and running with just a webcam and your high-speed internet connection. The HIPAA-compliant security measures ensure that your online sessions are fully-encrypted and confidential. Sessions may also be recorded and stored for future reference; and patient documentation can be downloaded in PDF format.

Cloud Visit Telehealth gives you instant access to patients, regardless of location. Video sessions let you control your schedule and help reduce office expenses.

We make it easy for you to leverage video chat technology in a way that is safe and secure. Our simple-to-use system lets you focus on your patients without having to learn complicated programs or worry about record keeping.

The benefits of online consultations

Saves time:

Video consultations give you the flexibility to treat patients from your home or office. You control the scheduling to fit within your regular in-office times or evening hours. Choosing Cloud Visit as your telehealth / telepsychiatry provider adds flexibility to your practice while allowing for better management of both your personal and professional time. The patients are happier, you are happier because you safe time and money. Money is saved from lack of travelling time and expense for the patient.

Grows Your Practice:

Having an online, or videoconferencing consultation can help you attract new patients, regardless of location, and increase profitable encounters with existing patients. By choosing Cloud Visit as your telehealth / telepsychiatry provider a new avenue of marketing is available and opened to you with your unique practice website and online presence.

Pricing:

The low-cost, and simple setup lets the physician treat patients with your current broadband internet connection and webcam. The low cost is also recycled back to the consumer, and the healthcare system as a whole benefits from delivery of efficient, cost effective healthcare delivery. With no expensive equipment to buy and easy credit card billing, immediate return on investment is realized.

Ease of use for both you and your patients is one of the major benefits of choosing Cloud Visit as your telehealth / telepsychiatry provider.

Improved productivity

One of the ways of loosing revenue in healthcare is via no shows, and lateness. Video consults make it easy for patients to keep appointments regardless of the weather, changes in their schedule, or transportation issues. Knowing their support is just a click away helps save them time and money.

Using Cloud Visit for telehealth / telepsychiatry provider creates a smoother treatment process for providers, and patients. This results in higher patient satisfaction rates and increases the likelihood of patient return and patient referrals.

Patients comments about telemedicine

"It saves me time & money."

Without the expense and aggravation of traveling to and from your office, patients are more relaxed and get more out of therapy. Flexible scheduling helps them fit appointments in between meetings or even during early morning or evening hours.

"I can see the provider that's right for me."

Online care lets a patient choose you as their provider regardless of where they live. Referrals are optimized when patients don't have to worry about you being too far away.

Choosing Cloud Visit as your telehealth provider gives you the unique advantage of having your own telehealth practice website, making you stand out from the crowd.

"It's so easy!"

Patients love hassle-free appointment scheduling and no-travel online consultations. They can stay home or simply close their office door and begin a session.

"Appointments are easy to keep."

No need to skip appointments when patients are feeling under the weather or stuck home due to poor road conditions. Video sessions help maintain continuous, obstacle-free care.

"It's affordable."

Patients appreciate the easy credit card payments and the ability to schedule individual or routine sessions.

Cloud Visit Telemedicine is committed to providing our clients with easy-to-use telehealth & telepsychiatry software services and solutions. For more information on how we can help grow your practice please call us at: **888-503-3009**. (2013 Aurora Software Technology, Inc., DBA Cloud Visit Telemedicine, retrieved 11/1/2013)

DEFINITION OF TERMS

AORN: Association of Perioperative Registered Nurses
ATA: American Telemedicine Association
BPHC: Bureau of Primary Health Care
CCHP: Center for Connected Health Policy
CHF: congestive heart failure

Cloud computing is an expression used to describe a variety of *computing* concepts that involve a large number of computers connected through a real-time communication network such as the Internet. In science, cloud computing is a synonym for distributed computing over a network and means the ability to run a program or application on many connected computers at the same time. The phrase also more commonly refers to network-based services, which appear to be provided by real server hardware, and are in fact served up by virtual hardware, simulated by software running on one or more real machines. Such virtual servers do not physically exist and can therefore be moved around and scaled up (or down) on the fly without affecting the end user—arguably, rather like a cloud.

The popularity of the term can be attributed to its use in marketing to sell hosted services in the sense of application service provisioning that run client server software on a remote location.

Community Setting Studies: These are studies conducted in home care, clinics, and physician offices.
Consumers: The patients who receive care from the health-care providers.
CMS. Center for Medicare/Medicaid Services
Distant Site: This is the site where the practitioner providing the professional service is located.
DHHS: Department of Health and Human Services
DHSS: Department of Health and Social Services
DOD: Department of Defense
e-Health, a.k.a. Electronic Health: This is the system of getting health care via electronic equipment.

This could be via e-mail, health buddy, or videoconferencing.

EHR: This is electronic health record. This is the current terminology for a digital patient's record.

e-Medicine: This is the term used to describe the practice of medicine from a distant site via electronic devices.

e-Visit: This is the term used to describe the e-mail communication between a physician and a patient. The patient describes his or her symptoms and the physician e-mails back his or her diagnosis of the symptoms described and recommends treatment.

ER: emergency room

Experimental Group: This is the group that participated in the experiment, or the group that used the product that is being tested.

FSMB: Federation of State Medical Boards

Health Buddy: This is a machine that downloads health questions for the clients every day, and the client answers the questions and gets feedback to their answers via the machine.

HHA: Home Health Aide. These are auxiliary staff that help the patients in performing activities of daily living, like showering, bathing, assistance with feeding, light housekeeping, and shopping.

HITC: Health Information Technology Coordinator

HHS: Health and Human Services

HIPAA: Health Insurance Portability and Accountability Act

HPSA: Health Professional Shortage Areas

HRSA: Health Resources and Services Administration

IHS: Institute for Human Services

Institutional Setting Studies: Institutional setting studies are studies conducted in hospitals, correction facilities, nursing homes, etc.

JCAHO: Joint Commission on Accreditation of Healthcare Organization

JWGT: Joint Working Group on Telehealth

MSW: Medical social workers. These are master's-prepared medical social workers who assess and manage the psychosocial well-being of patients, in collaboration with the primary physicians and other health-care professionals.

NCSBN: National Council of State Board of Nursing

NIH: National Institutes of Health

NLCA: Nurse licensure compact administrator. This is an administrator whose job is to facilitate the exchange of information between the states regarding compact nurse licensure and regulation.

NTIA: National Telecommunications and Information Administration

OAT: Office for the Advancement of Telehealth

Originating Site: The site where the patient is located at the time the service is provided.

POTS: Plain old telephone system. This is a simple way of transmitting telehealth information via a regular telephone line.

PT/ PTT: This is a special blood test used to monitor the thickness of the blood and how fast it clots.

Real Time: This is a system whereby the information entered into the telehealth unit is transmitted and received within seconds.

RPM: Remote patient monitoring

Store and Forward: This is a system where the telehealth unit sends its information to a storage center and the batched information is stored and forwarded to a designated center at a planned, scheduled time.

Telehealth Care Providers: These are the professionals, such as physicians, registered nurses, pharmacists, social workers, physical therapists, psychotherapists, etc., who deliver care to the consumers via telehealth

Telehealth Coordinators: These are the people responsible for coordinating and promoting telehealth or telehealth-related activities. The coordinators will answer telehealth or telehealth-related questions, interact with the telehealth companies on behalf of the staff, and assist in monitoring the general progress of the telehealth project.

Telehealth or Telemedicine: This is broadly defined as the use of telecommunication technologies, such as telephones, fax machines, computers, robots, video, etc., to deliver care and communicate between health-care givers and recipients in different or remote locations.

Telerobotic: This is the term used to describe the delivery of health care by a robot that is controlled from a distant location.

Telerobotic surgery: This is the term used to describe the performance of surgery by a robot that is controlled from a distant location.

Telerobotic: This is a form of telehealth or electronic health-care delivery where a robot performs a health-care task while being operated from a distance.

Telementoring: This is the term used to describe the process of talking a person through a procedure from a distant location.

Telepsychiatry: This is a system of practicing psychiatry from a different location via the use of telehealth tools.

Below are examples of telepsychiatric practices set up.

Contact number is 888-503-3009

Connecting with patients in a new way, the telepsychiatric way.

Online video sessions help physicians and institutions to grow their practice and revenue, while helping patients to obtain care at the comfort of their home, or while away.

Cloud Visit Connect is the easiest and most affordable telepsychiatry plan for private physicians and institutions to set up.

Set up is quick, and contract-free. It takes the worry out of seeing patients online. It is a win, win for patients and providers.

Types of CLOUD VISITS:

Cloud Visit-PRIVATE PRACTICE

Cloud Visit Private Practice bundles secure telepsychiatry tools into your own website. Perfect for any size practice!

Cloud Visits-INSTITUTION

On-site patient care is easy and safe with Cloud Visit Institution. Online sessions eliminate the need for provider travel, while giving patients access to the specialized care they need.

Our 3 easy, affordable telepsychiatry options fit the way you treat patients. With unlimited telepsychiatry in every plan, the sky's the limit.

Patient data under lock and key

HIPAA compliance and patient privacy are our top priorities. With the latest in data encryption, distributed servers, and enterprise-class webhosting, Cloud Visit is an information fortress.

We'll give you our written word that every piece of information you and your patients share through Cloud Visit is fully protected. Partner with Cloud Visit for HIPAA-compliant telehealth you can trust.

With Cloud Visit, all you need is:

- A computer
- A webcam with a microphone
- A broadband network

*Requires a download speed of 768Kb/sec and an upload speed of 384Kb/sec; connection of 2Mb down/1Mb up is suggested and for higher quality user experience

Cloud Visit Telemedicine is committed to providing our clients with easy-to-use telehealth & telepsychiatry software services and solutions. For more information on how we can help grow your practice please call us at: **888-503-3009**.

© 2013 Aurora Software Technology, Inc. DBA Cloud Visit Telemedicine. All Rights Reserved. Medical Website Design by Aurora IT.

Telepsychology: This is a form of telephone conference between a psychologist and a client. A complete session is done without face-to-face contact.

Teledermatology: This is a system whereby a dermatologist at a different location uses a telehealth tool to interact and diagnose a dermatological condition and recommend treatment.

TIE: Telemedicine Information Exchange. A newsletter with the latest information on telehealth.

Telepharmacy: This is a system where pharmacists are able to dispense medications and instructions via electronic and video equipment to patients.

VA: Veteran Administration

CONCLUSION

'On July 2014, California reps Mike Thompson, (D-CA) and Gregg Harper (R-MS) introduced a bill–dubbed the "Medicare Telehealth Parity Act of 2014". This bill–outlines a "phased-in" expansion of telehealth coverage over four years. Reimbursement would be expanded to include remote patient management services for chronic health conditions including congestive heart failure, chronic obstructive pulmonary disease and diabetes. It was stated that the guidelines for billing of such services would be determined by medical necessity.

These services will include in-home technology based professional consultations, patient monitoring, patient training services, clinical observation, assessment, treatment and any other services that utilize technologies. The above announcement is a welcomed news to the telehealth community. With forward thinking bills as noted above, consumers should be part of this moving force that encourages telehealth companies to be user friendly. Consumers should take front roll in the conversation alley. They should be active in taking surveys and speaking up regarding their experiences, pin point issues and systems that creates road block in navigating specific programs, and patronize companies that listen and implement change. By so doing, we will all encourage progress. As the debate continues, our nation and the world are challenged to think out of the box. We need to be bold and be realistic about the future of health care in our nation and the global health care. We are not alone in this journey. We need to take solace in the fact that the world is ready for a change in delivery of health care. The changes that are being demanded are as follow:

- Affordable healthcare
- Care Coordinated healthcare
- Care Management Healthcare
- Cost effective healthcare
- Culturally competent healthcare
- Just in time healthcare
- Population Management healthcare
- Quality Healthcare
- Safe and secure healthcare
- Self participatory healthcare

- Specialty Healthcare
- User friendly healthcare
- Value added healthcare.

All of the above are deliverable via Tele-health/Telemedicine, or Electronic health. Based on the above, I consider Tele-health/Telemedicine, or Electronic health a no brainer when appropriately mastered and managed. Ready or not, Telehealth is a mode of healthcare delivery system that is here to stay.

RESOURCES

1.)   Ahrq. Retrieved 10/28/2013. www.ahrq.org.

2.)   AMC Health. www.amchealth.com.

3.)   American Telemedicine Association. Retrieved 11/02/2013. *http://www.americantelemed.org/Healthinsight.gov.*

4.)   Athenahealth. Retrieved 11/10/2013. *http://www.athenahealth.com/.*

5.)   Aurora Software Technology, Inc. DBA Cloud Visit Telemedicine. Medical website design by Aurora IT. 2013.

6.)   Canadian Society of Tele-health. Retrieved 11/05/2013.

7.)   Castelli, Diane, RN, MS, MSN. Global Telemedicine, Inc. Retrieved 10/1/2013.

8.)   Center for Consumer Information and Insurance Oversight. Retrieved 10/30/2013.

9.)   CloudVisit Telemedicine. *http:///*Retrieved 1/21/2014. www.cloudvisittm.com.

10.)   HealthyChildren. Retrieved 1/20/2014. www.healthychildren.org.

11.)   Illinois Hospital Report Card and Consumer Guide to Health Care. Retrieved 11/04/2013 and 11/09/2013. *www.healthcarereportcard.illinois.gov.*

12.)   *Indiatimes.* October 29, 2013. *www.indiantimes.indiantimes.com.*

13.)   "Informed decision about your care." NYU Langone Medical Center. Retrieved 10/20/2013. http://med.nyu.edu/.

14.)   "International Competencies for Tele-nursing." International Council of Nurses. Retrieved 10/27/2013.

15.)   International Society for Telemedicine and e-Health. Retrieved 11/02/2013.

16.)   Kerouac, Jack. 2004. Generation Beat.

17.)   Makela, S., 2004. "Telecommunications in Health Care." JCAHO Standard regarding Tele-health, Tele-health at Marquette General Health System, pp. 1-2.

18.)   NetSquared. www.netsquared.org.

19.)   Northwestern Memorial Hospital. Retrieved 10/28/2013. www.nmh.org.

20.)   NYC Teen. Retrieved 11/2/2013.

21.)   The Office of Minority Health. Retrieved 10/28/2013. *http://minorityhealth.hhs.gov/templates/browse.aspx?lvl=3&lvlid=23.*

22.)   Ricci, Michael, Caputo Michael et al. 2004. "Tele-medicine Reduces Discrepancies in Rural Trauma." Tele-medicine journal and e-Health.

23.)   Rosen, E. 2002. "Eleven Minutes in the Life of a Tele-Home Health Nurse." In *Tele-Health Today.* Retrieved 8/20/2004.

24.) Spaulding, Ryan J. 2004. "Patient Satisfaction: Are patients who have used telemedicine satisfied with their experiences with it as a method of health care delivery?" Office of Advancement of Tele-health. Center for Telemedicine and Tele-health.

25.) State Telemedicine Policy Matrix. American Telemedicine Association. http://www.americantelemed.org/docs/default-source/policy/state-telemedicine-legislation-matrix.pdf.

26.) Telemedicine Information Exchange. Retrieved 10/20/2013.

27.) *Today's Parent.* Retrieved 10/07/2013 and 11/10/2013. *http://www.todaysparent.com/.*

28.) University of Oklahoma Bioengineering Center. http://www.oubc.ou.edu.

29.) UW Medicine. http://www.uwmedicine.org/.

30.) Washington, DC: National Academy Press.

INDEX

DATE DUE

Made in the USA
San Bernardino, CA
05 December 2015